STRANGERS WITHIN

( ) ( )

Published by Prototype in 2022
Reprinted in 2025

prototype publishing
71 oriel road
london e9 5sg
uk

admin@prototypepublishing.co.uk
www.prototypepublishing.co.uk
@prototypepubs

Edited by Therese Henningsen & Juliette Joffé

Copyright © Prototype Publishing
& individual contributors, 2022

Cover image © Susu Laroche

All rights reserved

No part of this publication may be reproduced, stored in a retrieval system, or transmitted, in any form or by any means, electronic, mechanical, photocopying, recording or otherwise, without the prior permission of the publishers.

Design by Theo Inglis
Typeset in Univers and ITC Avant Garde Gothic
Printed in the UK by Short Run Press

A CIP record for this book is available from the British Library

ISBN: 978-1-913513-30-6

This book has been generously supported by the Danish Arts Foundation, Flanders Literature and the Humanities and Arts Research Institute (HARI) at Royal Holloway, University of London, and Necessity.

( )   (   )
p   prototype

(type 4 // anthologies)

STRANGERS WITHIN

DOCUMENTARY AS ENCOUNTER

ED. THERESE HENNINGSEN
& JULIETTE JOFFÉ

( ) (   )

CONTENTS

Therese Henningsen & Juliette Joffé   7
Preface: Documentary as Encounter

Toni Morrison Strangers   17

Jon Bang Carlsen The Image of the Village   23
trans. Denise Rose Hansen

Ruth Beckermann In Praise of Detours   37
trans. David Perrin

Khalik Allah There's a Strength in Defencelessness   43

Annie Ernaux Towards a Transpersonal 'I'   55
trans. Dawn M. Cornelio

Jane Fawcett Freighted Curriculum, and My Family and Landscape: An Inheritance in the Flesh   61

Andrea Luka Zimmerman Don't Play with That Girl   65

Umama Hamido Pepe Pepe Pepe   79

Trinh T. Minh-ha Other Than Myself / My Other Self   95

Xiaolu Guo Woman with a Movie Camera   123

Juliette Joffé A Long-Forgotten Image   133

David MacDougall The Strangers within Us   141

Therese Henningsen All These Summers	161
Marc Isaacs The Lens as Shelter	177
Gareth Evans Strangerhood: On the Art of Oliver Bancroft	193
Mary Jiménez Freeman-Morris Gordon's Face Deal	209
Andrew & Eden Kötting Prick Me with Your Calamity, Wind Me with Your Familiarity	215
Bruno De Wachter Single Ticket *trans. Patrick Lennon*	241
Adam Christensen The Red Dream	257
Xiaolu Guo The Mystery of Language	265
Mireille Gansel Epilogue: comme une lettre	269
Contributor Biographies	274
Filmography	282
Acknowledgements	285

PREFACE: DOCUMENTARY AS ENCOUNTER

THERESE HENNINGSEN & JULIETTE JOFFÉ

I try to understand the intensity of my chagrin, and why I am missing a woman I spoke to for fifteen minutes ... Now she is gone, taking away with her my good opinion of myself, which, of course, is unforgivable. Isn't that the kind of thing that we fear strangers will do? Disturb. Betray. Prove they are not like us. That is why it is so hard to know what to do with them.
— Toni Morrison

In her text 'Strangers', written in 1998 and reproduced here, Toni Morrison is both enlivened and disturbed by an encounter with a fisherwoman – a stranger – whom she names Mother Something. The temporary presence of Mother Something, and their conversation – lasting merely fifteen minutes – leaves an indelible impression. The fisherwoman announces that she will return but does not, and is nowhere to be found. Her disappearance provokes conflicting responses: betrayal, fascination, obsession. She becomes an object of Morrison's projections, a cause for either false alarm or reverence. On reflection, Morrison realises that these emotions are provoked by a fear of the stranger within herself. This echoes with the title of this anthology, borrowed from Julia Kristeva. Kristeva proposes that we discover our own disturbing otherness by our projective apparition of the other at the heart of our attempts to maintain a 'solid' us. Accepting the difference within ourselves, she says, is the ultimate condition of our being *with* others.[1]

Kristeva's definition of the stranger within felt resonant when, two years ago, we first talked about putting together a screening programme focusing on the relational possibilities of the documentary encounter. The idea grew from a conversation we had about two of our own films: *Slow Delay* (2018), based on Therese's chance encounter with the elderly twins Trevor and Raymond, and *Next Year We Will Leave* (2021), a reconciliation with Juliette's hometown, Paris, through a dialogue with strangers. We talked about how they, although differently, shared a sense that the encounter with the person(s) – strangers – filmed spilled beyond the screen, directly affecting our own lives in the making. We wondered whether this is always the case in any type of filmmaking process.

This question led us to further reflect on the interrelations between encounters, hospitality and autobiography. Encounters, particularly with an emphasis on the unexpected and non-predetermined encounter and its relationship to filmmaking processes. Hospitality, inspired by Jacques Derrida's two lectures on hospitality, held at the École Pratique des Hautes Études in Paris in 1996. In 'Foreigner Question' and 'Step of Hospitality / No Hospitality', Derrida considers hospitality as a question of what arrives at the borders in the initial surprise of contact with an other, a stranger, a foreigner.[2] Autobiography, with an emphasis on exploring a personal cinema where the first-person narrative echoes the stories of those filmed.

The screening programme kept being delayed, and instead what was initially conceived as an associated pamphlet gradually grew into a work of its own – this anthology. We researched the works of filmmakers, writers and artists that resonated with the idea of 'the stranger within'. While our initial impulse concentrated on an exploration of filmmaking processes, we felt compelled to include writers and artists whose work – albeit in discrete ways – spoke to our concerns: Annie Ernaux, Toni Morrison, Adam Christensen, Jane Fawcett, Bruno De Wachter, Gareth Evans.

While encountering others in documentary processes is almost always (by its very nature) unpredictable, predeterminations of a question, an idea, a concept are often palpably felt. Projections onto those filmed are common (if not unavoidable), whether through logically arriving at certain narratives or through interpretations of people's life experiences. If a person does or thinks 'this', it must mean 'that'.

In both the physical and social sciences, suggests anthropologist and filmmaker David MacDougall, intentions are generally favoured. You need to have an idea of the direction of your research and of your main question, otherwise you merely have a muddle of undirected interests. The outcome can often be predicted from the questions asked, and the work serves to test conclusions already guessed at. Occasionally this opens up a completely new line of inquiry, but this is seen as exceptional rather than part of the original intention. MacDougall instead proposes 'dislocation as method'. In this approach, expectations may be upset, revised or superseded, and objectives recast by particular experiences:

> Here the outcome is unpredictable and open to sudden shifts of direction. To work in this way often means entrusting yourself to strangers and there is always the risk of becoming a stranger yourself ... For the filmmaker it is more than a calculated risk: it is a voluntary act of dislocation.[3]

MacDougall reminds us how letting go of our preconceptions involves an element of risk. When filmmakers are not sure what to think and not sure of the direction an encounter may take, the process becomes guided by uncertainty and doubt. Not trying to dominate or shy away from the unknown requires trust in the discovery process.

Addressing the making of her films *Estate, a Reverie* (2015) and *Here for Life* (2019), Andrea Luka Zimmerman describes the value of an approach that embraces the unfinished and the clumsy; of going on a yet-to-be-defined journey with the people filmed. With each new film, she suggests, there is a need to see in a way that is as yet unknown. Wandering and drifting is also welcomed in Ruth Beckermann's *Those Who Go Those Who Stay* (2013), in which she sets out to make a film with an intentionally unintentional gaze. This takes her on an unexpected journey across Europe and the

Mediterranean; an embodiment of her suggestion that every detour changes the destination.

Caught between two worlds (or more), filmmaker and writer Trinh T. Minh-ha's approach to autobiography values movement and journey and accommodates the exploration of our multiple selves. As a stranger to a new environment, everything safe and sound is destabilised. Trinh speaks of a voyage out of a known self back into the unknown self. The self loses its fixed boundaries – a disturbing yet potentially empowering practice of difference. There's a strength in defencelessness, advises photographer and filmmaker Khalik Allah, and in laying down your armour. In *IWOW: I Walk on Water* (2020), filmed mainly on the corner of 125th Street and Lexington Avenue in Harlem, New York City, he engages in a filmmaking process guided by chance encounters and by his ongoing friendship with the homeless Haitian man Frenchie. He explains how whenever he meets another person he is also meeting a part of himself. Here, the autobiographical meets the to-be-shared biography of the subject.

Seen this way, the filmic encounter could be interpreted as a hospitable act on both sides of the camera, allowing for a shared experience: the filmed welcomes the maker into their life, and, in turn, the lens becomes a temporary shelter for the filmed. In his interview about *The Filmmaker's House* (2020), filmmaker Marc Isaacs points out that 'camera' means 'room' in Latin. To film someone is also to welcome them into a tangible or intangible space: one's gaze, one's house or life. The porosity between 'life space' and 'filmic space' opens to a wider question: can or should the encounter with the other through film change the maker's life? Like any encounter, it has the power to do so. In *Far and Near* (2003), writer and filmmaker Xiaolu Guo meets people in rural Wales whose differences from and similarities to herself allow her to reflect on her own life and journey.

Yet strict boundaries are often palpable when filming another and tend to separate the spaces behind and in front of the camera.

Jean Rouch argues that the filmic encounter is like no other: the camera acts as a psychoanalytic stimulant on the filmed, who opens up in a way they would not otherwise have done.[4] The power of the camera and the gaze is illustrated by Marilou Parolini's vulnerability when confiding her feelings of loneliness and depression to sociologist Edgar Morin in *Chronicle of a Summer* (1961), Rouch's seminal documentary made in collaboration with Morin. Welcoming someone into one's gaze always implies a power relation. The gaze, as we know, holds an insistent potential as an agent of control.

Trinh memorably proposes a distinction between 'speaking nearby' and 'speaking about': to speak nearby implies an open gaze, one that does not impose itself on the other or seek to ignore the space between maker and subject. Instead, it lets them 'come in and fill that space as they wish'. She continues:

> By not trying to assume a position of authority in relation to the other, you are actually freeing yourself from the endless criteria generated with such an all-knowing claim and its hierarchies in knowledge.[5]

Film is necessarily a relational medium. What does it mean for filmmakers to let go of their position of authority to adopt one of openness and vulnerability, one that allows them to be affected by the other beyond the strictly defined 'filmic space'? Uncertainty of direction and outcome are often feared by producers and funders, who favour clarity and solidity of structure. However, if a substantial space is given to the filmed other it can give them the freedom to change the planned course of events, to alter not only the film but even, beyond it, the filmmaker's life and self.

Danish director Jon Bang Carlsen's film *Addicted to Solitude* (1999) begins with a statement of failure: his initial intention for the film proved impossible to realise, which left him stranded in a small village with nothing to do but meet some of the few inhabitants of the place. As he sits and waits, he meets two women who, like himself, spend most of their time waiting: for a loved one or for a customer to come. Silence fills the room. In moments when 'nothing happens', the shop owner offers brief glimpses of inner truths, which resonate with Carlsen's own life. In these fragile moments, they bond over a shared feeling of solitude.

In this process of identification, time spent with the other with no specific intention apart from sharing time plays an important role. *On Akka's Shore* (2018) by artist Umama Hamido is constructed around long-term sound recordings of conversations with her friend Jaz (Tareq Al Jazzar). Scenes slip between Akka in Palestine; a Palestinian refugee camp in Lebanon; Beirut, Hamido's city of birth; and London, their current home. Their dialogue and shared time is the source material of the film – an extension of life. They both occupy a place in-between – neither here nor there, or both here and there. Jaz's experience of hallucinations and Umama's own dreams blend into a shared fictional memoir across the borders of selves.

In her text reproduced here, writer Annie Ernaux speaks of a 'transpersonal *I*'. 'The *I* that I use', she writes, seems an 'impersonal form, barely gendered, sometimes even a word belonging more to "the other" than to "me": a transpersonal form'. Hers is an *I* that acknowledges how individual and collective experiences intertwine. In the preface to her book *Journal du dehors* ('Diary of the Outside', 2013), she writes: 'I am sure, now, that we learn even more about ourselves when we go out into the world than in the introspection of the private diary.' In her reading of Ernaux, writer Lauren Elkin suggests that the self is not contained within our minds and bodies, but distributed across all the places we have been to and the people with whom we have crossed paths.[6]

Trinh reminds us how the self can take in as many identities as there are encounters in one's life. She proposes an alternative understanding of a reflexive cinema – not as a 'narrative of self-location as a solution', but reflexive on all levels at once: 'between maker, viewer and viewed; between diverse elements of the cinematic fabric'. In these limitless reflections between people, things, moments and events, we can explore relationships in their differences and multiplicities. She offers a welcome view on the possibilities of the filmic encounter:

> Each encounter is utterly bound to the elements that define it [and] the specificity of each encounter would dictate a different course for each film. Each film having its own field of energies, the unique form it takes on in the process remains non-predetermined.[7]

Further meditating on her encounter with Mother Something, Morrison reasons that by governing and administering the other, we deny her personhood – the specific individuality we insist upon for ourselves. This echoes with a call for probing the complexities of engaging without governing, both in filmmaking and in life. In this anthology, we explore works where the camera may be seen as an agent of encounter, and where the filmed is not merely a 'subject' but a person entering the life of the maker, whose presence might unsettle both their gaze and self-perception. Employing the idea of the 'stranger within' across essay, story and interview, the texts contained here engage with the relational and reflective potential of the filmic (and life) encounter.

Therese Henningsen and Juliette Joffé
London / Brussels / Aarhus, May 2022

1 Julia Kristeva, *Strangers to Ourselves* (New York: Columbia University Press, 1991), p. 192.
2 Jacques Derrida and Anne Dufourmantelle, *Of Hospitality*, trans. Rachel Bowlby (Stanford, CA: Stanford University Press, 2000).
3 David MacDougall, *The Looking Machine: Essays on Cinema, Anthropology and Documentary Filmmaking* (Manchester: Manchester University Press, 2019), p. 10.
4 Michael Renov, *The Subject of Documentary* (Minneapolis, MN: University of Minnesota Press, 2004), p. 127.
5 Erika Balsom, '"There is No Such Thing as Documentary": An Interview with Trinh T. Minh-ha', *Frieze* 199, www.frieze.com, 1 November 2018.
6 Lauren Elkin, 'Encountering Annie Ernaux's Urban Landscapes and Scattered Selves', https://lithub.com, 16 September 2021.
7 Trinh T. Minh-ha, 'Inside and Outside the Abyss (Tuning into Edouard Glissant)', foreword to Édouard Glissant and Hans Ulrich Obrist, *Isolarii #6: The Archipelago Conversations* (2021).

STRANGERS
TONI MORRISON

I am in this river place – newly mine – walking in the yard when I see a woman sitting on the seawall at the edge of a neighbor's garden. A homemade fishing pole arcs into the water some twenty feet from her hand. A feeling of welcome washes over me. I walk toward her, right up to the fence that separates my place from the neighbor's, and notice with pleasure the clothes she wears: men's shoes, a man's hat, a well-worn colorless sweater over a long black dress. The woman turns her head and greets me with an easy smile and a 'How you doing?' She tells me her name (Mother Something) and we talk for some time – fifteen minutes or so – about fish recipes and weather and children. When I ask her if she lives there, she answers no. She lives in a nearby village, but the owner of the house lets her come to this spot any time she wants to fish, and she comes every week, sometimes several days in a row when the perch or catfish are running and even if they aren't because she likes eel, too, and they are always there. She is witty and full of the wisdom that older women always seem to have a lock on. When we part, it is with an understanding that she will be there the next day or very soon after and we will visit again. I imagine more conversations with her. I will invite her into my house for coffee, for tales, for laughter. She reminds me of someone, something. I imagine a friendship, casual, effortless, delightful.

She is not there the next day. She is not there the following days, either. And I look for her every morning. The summer passes, and I have not seen her at all. Finally, I approach the neighbor to ask about her and am bewildered to learn that the neighbor does not know who or what I am talking about. No old woman fished from her wall – ever – and none had permission to do so. I decide that the fisherwoman fibbed about the permission and took advantage of the neighbor's frequent absences to poach. The fact of the neighbor's presence is proof that the fisherwoman would not be there. During the months following, I ask lots of people if they know Mother Something.

No one, not even people who have lived in nearby villages for seventy years, has ever heard of her.

I feel cheated, puzzled, but also amused, and wonder off and on if I have dreamed her. In any case, I tell myself, it was an encounter of no value other than anecdotal. Still. Little by little, annoyance then bitterness takes the place of my original bewilderment. A certain view from my windows is now devoid of her, reminding me every morning of her deceit and my disappointment. What was she doing in that neighborhood, anyway? She didn't drive, had to walk four miles if indeed she lived where she said she did. How could she be missed on the road in that hat, those awful shoes? I try to understand the intensity of my chagrin, and why I am missing a woman I spoke to for fifteen minutes. I get nowhere except for the stingy explanation that she had come into my space (next to it, anyway – at the property line, at the edge, just at the fence, where the most interesting things always happen), and had implied promises of female camaraderie, of opportunities for me to be generous, of protection and protecting. Now she is gone, taking with her my good opinion of myself, which, of course, is unforgivable.

Isn't that the kind of thing that we fear strangers will do? Disturb. Betray. Prove they are not like us. That is why it is so hard to know what to do with them. The love that prophets have urged us to offer the stranger is the same love that Jean-Paul Sartre could reveal as the very mendacity of Hell. The signal line of 'No Exit', *'L'enfer, c'est les autres'*,[1] raises the possibility that 'other people' are responsible for turning a personal world into a public hell. In the admonition of a prophet and the sly warning of an artist, strangers as well as the beloved are understood to tempt our gaze, to slide away or to stake claims. Religious prophets caution against the slide, the looking away; Sartre warns against love as possession.

The resources available to us for benign access to each other, for vaulting the mere blue air that separates us, are few but powerful: language, image, and experience, which may involve both, one, or neither of the first two. Language (saying, listening, reading) can encourage, even mandate, surrender, the breach of distances among us, whether they are continental or on the same pillow, whether they are distances of culture or the distinctions and indistinctions of age or gender, whether they are the consequences of social invention or biology. Image increasingly rules the realm of shaping, sometimes becoming, often contaminating, knowledge. Provoking language or eclipsing it, an image can determine not only what we know and feel but also what we believe is worth knowing about what we feel.

These two godlings, language and image, feed and form experience. My instant embrace of an outrageously dressed fisherwoman was due in part to an image on which my representation of her was based. I immediately sentimentalized and appropriated her. I owned her or wanted to (and I suspect she glimpsed it). I had forgotten the power of embedded images and stylish language to seduce, reveal, control. Forgot, too, their capacity to help us pursue the human project – which is to remain human and to block the dehumanization of others.

But something unforeseen has entered into this admittedly oversimplified menu of our resources. Far from our original expectations of increased intimacy and broader knowledge, routine media presentations deploy images and language that narrow our view of what humans look like (or ought to look like) and what in fact we are like. Succumbing to the perversions of media can blur vision, resisting them can do the same. I was clearly and aggressively resisting such influences in my encounter with the fisherwoman. Art as well as the market can be complicit in the sequestering of form from formula, of nature from artifice, of humanity from commodity. Art gesturing toward representation has, in some exalted quarters, become literally beneath contempt. The concept of what it is to be human has altered, and the word *truth* needs quotation marks around it so that its absence (its elusiveness) is stronger than its presence.

Why would we want to know a stranger when it is easier to estrange another? Why would we want to close the distance when we can close the gate? Appeals in arts and religion for comity in the Common Wealth are faint.

It took some time for me to understand my unreasonable claims on that fisherwoman. To understand that I was longing for and missing some aspect of myself, and that there are no strangers. There are only versions of ourselves, many of which we have not embraced, most of which we wish to protect ourselves from. For the stranger is not foreign, she is random, not alien but remembered; and it is the randomness of the encounter with our already known – although unacknowledged – selves that summons a ripple of alarm. That makes us reject the figure and the emotions it provokes – especially when these emotions are profound. It is also what makes us want to own, govern, administrate the Other. To romance her, if we can, back into our own mirrors. In either instance (of alarm or false reverence), we deny her personhood, the specific individuality we insist upon for ourselves.

Robert Bergman's radiant portraits of strangers provoked this meditation. Occasionally, there arises an event or a moment that one knows immediately will forever mark a place in the history of artistic endeavor. Bergman's portraits represent such a moment, such an event. In all its burnished majesty his gallery refuses us unearned solace, and one by one by one the photographs unveil us, asserting a beauty, a kind of rapture, that is as close as can be to a master template of the singularity, the community, the unextinguishable sacredness of the human race.

—

1 French existentialist philosopher (1905–1980). The line in Sartre's 1944 play *No Exit* is usually translated as 'Hell is other people'.

THE IMAGE OF THE VILLAGE

JON BANG CARLSEN

TRANSLATED FROM THE DANISH
BY DENISE ROSE HANSEN

I was gifted a camera for my ninth birthday. My first photograph was of Dad and me. Sadly, he forgot to mention that I had to wind on the film before taking the next picture, and so his face disappeared behind some piano sheet music by Chopin.

That's how it was with Dad and me, something usually went wrong. But ever since he gave me that incredible gift, I've stared at the world through a camera ... maybe because I need to keep at a certain distance to focus the lens, and that's something those of us from remote villages excel at: keeping a distance.

In the sweet days of childhood, before Dad disappeared and Mum withdrew into an unyielding darkness, the village was little more than a series of pleasant weekdays that never brought anything into question. Wondering about the meaning of life was a waste of time, as our wise ancestors had already thought all the thoughts. I was simply to lean into their wisdom and rejoice that God and his Son wanted the best for me and my family.

When Dad, despite all my prayers, left us, I scorched out Jesus's eyes in the picture that Dad had hung above my bed. In an instant, that parochial world collapsed, and everything I had been sure of was now riddled with doubt. The village was the same, but I had suddenly become a stranger to it, and then it is all very well to retreat behind the camera and simply stare at all that is incomprehensible. The slow, tracking shot of dim houses, seen from a stranger's point of view as they pass along the single, long street of a village, appears in many of my films. It's as though this shot is the very first letter of my alphabet.

Now I was the stranger, and the solemn faces behind the curtains were leering out at me.

It was the beginning of a lifetime of drifting about the globe.

*

To evade the darkness that enclosed my mother, and to forget Jesus's scorched-out eyes, I decided to leave the village. The thought of, with time, being buried alive in one of those nondescript red-brick houses sent shivers down my spine. Perhaps that's why I, time and time again, had to move past suburban streets, dizzying myself with new horizons.

Hiding behind the camera, I had an alibi for drawing closer to other people's faces without revealing my own. I sought out faces that could inspire me to see life in new ways.

In Phoenix, Arizona, I met a Vietnam veteran and decided to find out if the struggle for survival in the jungles of Vietnam could be a way out of the deadly monotony of the village.

In Los Angeles, the extra Dan Pattarson confirmed my mother's idea that the only way to give reality wings is to turn it into a dream. The former butcher, who had fled Chicago for the City of Angels, became one of my many teachers. As did his neighbour further down the hotel hallway, who, unlike Pattarson, wasn't just fighting his roommate ... but the entire world.

And then there was Sir Ove Arup, the distinguished engineer in London, who like me had forgotten that which he wanted more than anything to remember. And in South Africa, I hired a young actress who stubbornly claimed that films carry on even after the camera stops.

We came from vastly different places across the globe, and yet we mirrored each other almost like brothers and sisters. The more faces my camera brought into focus, the more brothers and sisters I had – brothers and sisters who have all, through the years and in each their own way, shown me new roads out of the village.

Being constantly in motion without going anywhere is sort of ridiculous, but it became my way of breaking away from the everyday. Back home, Mrs Beck, the keeper of the village inn, had no plans to break away. To Mrs Beck, the village was the centre of the universe.

All across the world I've met people like the ones back home in my village. All of us wondering what our lives would have been like had we dared step into the unknown, which could be the love I myself had such a hard time believing in because it had hurt my family so much.

In my Danish village, small acts of affection had, curiously and over time, ousted the notion of great passion. Just as something was about to blossom, winter would come, and this cycle would repeat over and over. Maybe this is why I prefer to film people when they aren't in the thick of action but are merely carrying out the mundane tasks that make up a life. I've always found this incredibly hardcore: simply letting time pass, like it did in the village, nothing ever happening, just waiting untroubled for death. It's not for chickens.

I never accepted that I ought to feel at home in the exact place where Mum happened to push me out into the light. She could have given birth to me anywhere. Making a destiny out of an arbitrary location, simply because you happen to be born there, is absurd. But then we remote villagers are obsessed with the idea of a destiny. That chance may be the basic principle of life fills us with dread.

My mother could have given birth to me in a desert ... in the particular silence of a landscape that's far from the sea. When I visited such forsaken deserts, memories were the only rainwater on my face. People lost their gravity and became music. They lived inside me like a tune.

Now and then I had to look at myself in the rear-view mirror to make sure that I myself was still there in the flesh.

'Strange that only that which is not ... is ... and continues to be,' my mother once said moments before she drifted off to sleep, leaving me with yet another incomprehensible sentence from the world of adults.

While I meandered along distant highways, daily life in the village continued unperturbed, as though the rest of the world was little more than a *déjà vu* they'd long since figured out. How could they be so calm, merely letting time pass, for no better reason than reaching the end of the county road? It was baffling to me that the villagers, even during the Cuban Missile Crisis, were able to sleep on so soundly in their abysmal armchairs, when not only their world but the entire planet was teetering on the brink of nuclear annihilation.

While Mum tucked herself away in the red-brick house with her beloved opera, her restless son had to keep on moving, but luckily, Mum was fond of writing letters, and these sustained me mile after mile.

In flight away from the village, I met a group that I, for the first time since my family split up, wanted to be part of. A band of young actors who wanted to create a heaven here on earth.

Together with my new friends, I returned to my Danish village, this time disguised as an angel. My wings were so ridiculously short that we had to charter a helicopter in order to arrive in style. We kissed the mayor's hand, which still smelled of the pigs he had fed moments earlier, then approached the village dressed up like the dreams we imagined the villagers to dream in their quiet houses. One of our number in the guise of Ophelia, searching for her Danish prince.

Our goal was to make visible the dreams of the village for everyone to see and thereby encourage people to create their own reality. We wanted to show the village that the enemy is not those who doubt but those who claim that everyday life is immutable. So we attacked the everyday, with all the arms of the imagination we could muster. But the people of my mother's village didn't want to change – certainly didn't want to be made to change by me and my raucous friends from the big city. Or maybe it was me. Was I not still scared of the village's single, long street, and the darkness in my mother's eyes? So scared that I fled once again, angel wings under my arm.

East of the Iron Curtain, the old despots were being removed from their plinths. Like everyone else, I rushed with my camera to West Berlin to watch the infamous wall be torn down and past heroes vanish into darkness. But rather than filming the people cheering the fall of the wall, my camera fell in love with some dejected youths who lived in the rapidly diminishing wasteland between the two superpowers. Like the youths, I felt more at home in the no man's land than anywhere else, because in the no man's land no inflated, medal-adorned authorities decreed what was real and what wasn't.

*

In Los Angeles, I felt for the first time since the village that I could also have been born here. Maybe because the City of Angels was the vastest no man's land of them all. It was a relief for the village boy to find himself among fake angels, in a place where even reality was dressed up as a dream.

In the Hotel Montecito on Franklin Avenue, just across from Hollywood Boulevard, we hid ourselves and our flighty dreams away, so that those who were too faint of heart didn't drag us screeching back down to earth.

In the City of Angels, Jesus was just another movie star. In this giant, neon-lit village, where everything and nothing could happen, our identities changed all the time. Like the wealthy man who out of boredom left his mansion in Beverly Hills to live among the homeless.

It was quite popular among the rich to dress like they were poor, to experience on their own bodies what it might be like ... to be the complete opposite. Strangely enough, none of the poor ever pretended they were rich and invaded the lavish mansions of Beverly Hills.

Like the rich man, I drifted about the globe, perpetually searching for a magical place, where the throb of life was strong enough to appease the worry that we might be headed in the wrong direction.

The rich man had the money to stage his dreams. I had my camera, and it opened all the doors.

Although life was happening right there in front of my pointed camera, I had a hard time taking part in it. Maybe because the seasoned director knows how quickly those in front of the camera reveal their wounds ... willingly or not.

As a filmmaker, I relied so much on my eyes that I wasn't able to believe in something I couldn't see. So when one day I could no longer make out my own reflection, I was terrified that I had ended up like the stone face in the South Atlantic. That I was glaring up at a burnt-out sky I had long since lost the ability to actually see.

Seized by desperation, I hired a blind man to focus on all that me and my camera were no longer able to bring into focus. For months I filmed my blind friend, without ever figuring out how he was able to decode the world so infinitely more accurately than my own pedantic eyes.

When I turned nine my father gave me a camera, as I mentioned earlier, and since then I'd photographed everything and everyone. But more than half a century on, no matter what subject I focused on, it separated me from life rather than letting me into it. Maybe I was the blind one. And the believers I kept stalking with my camera, filming without understanding their faith, incapable as I was of believing in anything myself.

I was caught in a maelstrom of meaningless images and stupid questions. It went on like that, like a runaway train hurtling past all the stations at full speed. Eventually my incessant doubt had me interrupting my hard-working actors as they tried to breathe life into roles I myself had pedantically written for them yet had already started doubting.

Of course it was one of my old friends from the Hotel Montecito who tried to parse the large, childish letters that seemed written across my sweaty forehead. But unfortunately the man behind the camera had a tendency to feel smarter than the people in front of it, so I decided the bald man was talking about all sorts of idiots other than me. Things were as they had been for years ... even the most beautiful answers were drowned out by the noise of the questions.

'Do you believe in God?' asked an elderly woman in a small dusty town in South Africa many years later, when I once again had stumbled over my own questions. It was the first time anyone had asked the face *behind* the camera a question. Perhaps this was why I gave up continuing on my travels and just sat in the silence of her thrift shop for weeks while thinking of the people back home in the village, and of Jesus, who might again have eyes with which to see.

When I told the woman that as a child, grieving the collapse of my family, I had scorched out Jesus's eyes, she said that we cannot burn out the eyes of Jesus ... only our own.

I had reached a point where the question mark that was where my spine should be became too much to lug around. But every time I opened my mouth ... another question.

Later, a small church in Fanore on the western coast of Ireland became my new refuge. Another no man's land where people seemed to wait, in devout silence, for someone who might never come. Here I could wallow in my doubt, sheltered by the faith of others as they carried out the little rituals believers perform in order to bring their absent creator into focus.

Like the Irish farmer Jimmy, the main character in *It's Now or Never*, we all create our own image of the great absent father we've missed for an eternity. And the image depends on whether life has spoiled us with tenderness, or whether we struggle to feel something more than loneliness and the resentment that grows so fiercely in its shade.

The Vietnam veteran in *Phoenix Bird* inspired me to write a scene that grew out of the memory of the opulent flowers my mother would sometimes decorate her sitting room with, until her joy suddenly withered because she felt she had staged her own funeral. Later, in the film *Time Out*, I placed my mother's flowers in the hands of a little girl in Vietnam.

Back home in the village, no matter what happened in the world, Jenny kept on milking her cows ... for why cease doing what she could do in her sleep, what she had been doing since she was a little girl, even if her arthritic hands were telling her to stop?

*

Read another melancholy letter from my mother. Strange that I, through all those years meandering around the globe, never dared point the camera at the mirroring that had me flee my Danish village. The very first mirroring. The face I cannot put behind me ... the face of my mother.

Nothing ever happened when I was growing up. Until love suddenly blew up between the hands of my family and we all got hurt. Whatever happened later in my life, it always turned out to be connected with those modest, oddly abandoned houses, and the flat, barren fields with scattered farms hiding in the windswept landscape. To the pigs' convulsions when they squealed life goodbye, so that Jenny could have her roast pork every Christmas, clad in red, the practical woman that she was, so that the blood stains weren't so distinct.

My mother was not a practical woman like Jenny, and death wasn't a roast pork in the fridge to be enjoyed with the family. Death was the only pitiful remainder when love seeped out of life and everything lost its meaning ... even daily life with the son who kept coming and going, as though there was still some sort of method to the madness.

The saddening story about what happens between parents and their children when a family falls apart and meaninglessness starts spreading like weeds in an otherwise carefully tended garden ... wherever I found myself on this earth, my camera kept running across this story, because it was a story I recognised.

The invisible but painful scars of teenagers in American suburbia taught me that no matter how old we are, the wounds our parents inflicted on us never heal, and that we will never be wise enough to stop chasing the love we feel we are owed.

I returned to the white house in the suburbs. I'd filmed this beautiful house before, but the camera had never detected any life inside ... maybe the man who lived there had died years before ... but suddenly, there he was ... I haven't seen him in more than fifty years, and yet I am instantly back under his power the moment he opens the window ... and I panic and feel awfully miserable that I daren't show my face to the man I have missed all my life ... all I need to do is open my mouth and say 'Hello Dad' ... but I can't ... instead I pretend I'm a stranger obsessed with suburban streets.

When he closed the window, I felt the same desolation as all those years ago, when Dad had left the village for America and I disappeared from his life for good ... while he remained in mine ... like a phantom.

I never understood how he could leave us, as I've always believed that love can only survive when it's nurtured by both lovers.

The old man who probably had trouble sleeping that night in Los Angeles, and who suddenly caught sight of a suspicious middle-aged man loitering outside his house, was not my real father. He was just a reflection of something within me, something that needed a body which the camera could bring into focus. This is how we manipulate the world, professional liars in search of truth.

*

While I was preoccupied with staring at strangers' faces through my camera, a family was growing up around me, a family that saw no reason to hide behind a large, unblinking eye.

Fortunately, my sons were not afraid. Thanks to the restlessness of their parents, they had already travelled far more in their childhood than I had at their age. Travelling makes brave, as my blind friend used to say before he threw himself off a mountain.

Perhaps only love can give us glimpses of God. Perhaps love is the only crack through which we are allowed to look into Paradise without having our eyes scorched out. A divine peepshow. Maybe that's why 'God is love' is written both on the gravestones in South Africa and on those in the cemetery of my remote Danish village, and probably in cemeteries all around the world, no matter what *we* call the gods of others.

The love between the elderly couple in *First I Wanted to Find the Truth* was the kind of love my own parents ought to have experienced. Two people knitted together by the passage of time, as my wife and I have come to be. But even in the most symbiotic kind of love, both lovers know that one day they will have to let go of the other's hand and leave this world alone. Maybe that's why we need God – like a perennial post box into which we can drop our love letters, even when the address has become unknown.

The stone face in the Atlantic Ocean, staring up at the hazy, African sky trying to catch a glimpse of God, reminded me of myself. One of my sons drew invisible pictures on the windows with his friend, while my other son played 'who can stare the longest into the camera without blinking' with his. Finally it dawned on me how foolish it is to stare at the sky, trying to catch sight of God. God is something we can find only in each other, with everything we contain, the good and the bad. That's why I decided to return to my birthplace on the other side of the earth, and to the people I had grown up with.

When I had reached the remote village, greeted friends and foes, and laid a flower on my mother's grave, I finally realised that the villagers weren't hiding from the world. They just lived their lives without making things more difficult than they needed to be. The answer I'd been searching for through all those decades of travel had perhaps been right there in front of me, ever since I was born in that red-brick house on the village's single, long street. I asked Mrs Beck the most banal of questions: what did she find most beautiful about life? And for some reason that I will probably never understand, she only answered me after she'd stolen the light from my camera.

'To keep on living.'

Although for decades I have been moving away from the village's deafening silence, I am still created in its image. The image of the village is naïve in its simplicity. A straight road, which for a brief moment, as it passes by the low red-brick houses, is upgraded to a street, only to immediately and dutifully become a road again, leading the traveller towards the next village.

Despite all the questions I've put to unwitting people all over the world, I try to hold on to my childhood conviction that the reason the white stripes on the road become craggier with time is that they eventually reveal to the traveller what they really are: the long, white hairs of God's beard.

Now, the journey is over, and maybe I'll be able to regain a sense of calm in one of the red-brick houses. There may still be a harbour where all of us restless souls can dock, no matter how helter-skelter we have steered this way and that on our way across the water.

—

All of the films referenced here are available at jonbangcarlsen.com

IN PRAISE OF DETOURS

RUTH BECKERMANN

TRANSLATED FROM THE GERMAN
BY DAVID PERRIN

When I think about filming and travelling, I see trains or cars before me. The film strip and the strip of road or railway line – both born out of the same moment – are phenomena of the past. These days we fly to places and what was once called film is today a digital data product. Over the last thirty years, I have travelled across the different forms of film – from 16mm and 35mm to Mini DV and Full HD. Looking back, it's amazing to see not only how much the formats have changed, but also the changes in my perception and that of the viewer.

In *Towards Jerusalem* (1991), I still followed a road, in this case from the Mediterranean Sea to Jerusalem, in order to compare the myths and ideologies associated with Israel with what was really there. I wanted to squeeze myself into the narrowest possible path, a kind of corset that would prevent me from straying this or that way in order to find interesting people to film or from gathering evidence that would merely confirm my preconceived notions and desires. For five long weeks we moved up and down this 60-kilometre strip of road, filming a seemingly random slice of reality in Israel – which frequently resulted in surprises.

With *American Passages* (2011), I developed the travel film even further. Though the direction of our journey from east to west across the United States remained unchanged, here we hopped and skipped over the map and through the landscape. The faster you move, the more abstractly you see the world. *Those Who Go Those Who Stay* (2013) already shows an associative mode of travel. Some say the film is rooted in the so-called channel-hopping age. This may be, though what is channel-hopping other than a kind of search among the bookshelves whereby I leap from one book to another? Or surfing the Internet, that endless library, which can lead one down such wonderful detours. Channel-hopping is a form of fragmentation, a breaking-out of the analogue standard. Yet it is also a form of montage, meaning the creation of (new) relationships between things.

It is the montage that counts. As long as it lies within my hands, it will provide the audience with my sense of order. For this, we need the cinema, where no one can wield his or her remote control. The dark space and the narrow rows of seats force the audience to concentrate, taking them on a journey with the filmmaker as their travel guide.

Choosing to work within the framework of a journey means to explicitly be on the search for inner images that are to be projected into the outer world, and also, conversely, to arrive at a new inner order within foreign surroundings. But soon you realise that finding is better than searching. But how do you find what you were searching for, without searching? Not by way of a direct path, but perhaps through mental preparations and in dreams. Before shooting my film *The Paper Bridge* (1987) in Romania, I made a long wish list of scenes and images, all connected somehow to the world of the shtetl and the Hasidic tales of mythical rabbis and paper bridges that lead to a better world. It had to be winter, with a fog that diffused the present, thus creating a space where memories could unfold.

One of the images I wished for was of a horse and buggy slowly vanishing into the fog. In December we left Vienna, driving a VW Bus that was packed full with our equipment – camera, tripod, lighting equipment and film stock. We were hardly over the border, on a country road in Romania, when a horse and buggy appeared, enveloped in a thick fog. It was hard to believe. The cheers of joy! But we had to keep a cool head and act quickly. Stop the car. Break out the equipment. Firmly mount the tripod onto the roof of our vehicle, load the film into the camera and pursue. The desired image wants to be captured. Shooting documentaries is always stressful, because it's about capturing the right moment with every shot. Even when nothing happens, or you think that tomorrow is another day. No, tomorrow everything will be different. The sun will shine, and the buggy will be a gleaming carriage.

We are standing at a crossroads in Cairo, capturing the rhythm of the traffic moving in every possible direction. The scene itself can be banal or exciting, such as when a shaft of light illuminates three red cars; when the traffic light flashes green in front of the blue sky; and a passing truck enters the shot at precisely the right moment when three girls hesitantly attempt to cross the road. For that, one doesn't have to travel. Crossroads exist at home too. Yet it's the small differences, whether it be a donkey grazing on a traffic island, a police officer wildly gesturing with his long white gloves, or the concert of unfamiliar honking noises, that open our eyes and ears. Travelling makes you more alert, a state of mind that doesn't last long and that you must take advantage of. No preliminary research or surveys beforehand; instead, it's about looking, listening and shooting.

Victor Segalen defined exoticism as the 'aesthetics of diversity'. What one sees expresses the echo of one's own presence:

> Exoticism is therefore not the kaleidoscopic vision of the tourist or of the mediocre spectator, but the forceful and curious reaction to a shock felt by someone of strong individuality in response to some object whose distance from oneself he alone can perceive and savor ... Exoticism is therefore not an adaptation to something; it is not the perfect comprehension of something outside of one's self that one has managed to embrace fully, but the keen and immediate perception of an eternal incomprehensibility.[1]

One travels to remote places and journeys into the past. There are many parallels between the distance to the past and spatial distance. 'Perhaps the past is a faraway country,' I say in *A Fleeting Passage to the Orient*, and thus justify my decision to make a film about Empress Elisabeth of Austria in Egypt. A long detour, to be sure, but 'elsewhere' and 'what once was' are closer to each other than one thinks.

Making films and travelling means to move around in unsafe zones, to be always ready for surprises. To lose your way, to go astray in order to discover something that you could not foresee but is perhaps exactly what you were looking for. Every detour changes the destination.

—

1 Victor Segalen, *Essay on Exoticism: An Aesthetics of Diversity* (Durham, NC: Duke University Press, 2002), pp. 20–21.

THERE'S A STRENGTH IN DEFENCELESSNESS
—
KHALIK ALLAH

IN CONVERSATION WITH
THERESE HENNINGSEN

THERESE HENNINGSEN: I'm interested in talking about filmmaking as a form of encounter. I think your filmmaking is very much a process that is led by the encounters you have with the people you film. And so, to start with that question, I'd like to know if you see your filmmaking as a form of encounter and, if so, how?

KHALIK ALLAH: Sure. I would say that I do documentary work and it's unpredictable. There are many people that I stop in the street and it's just that: it's an encounter, there's a level of communication that is unpredictable. I think that's also what makes it interesting. I'm not even sure what I'm going to say in that encounter, and I'm not sure what the reaction is going to be – to me filming, or to the questions I may pose. So the work is definitely a form of encounter, but my personal attitude is that whenever I meet a person, I'm meeting a part of myself. I don't see the encounter as encountering somebody that's separate from me. My work is very much about identifying myself in the other, in the other person. My work is about empathy and showing that there is a relationship between artist and subject.

So it definitely is an encounter; I would say it's a loving encounter. It's a respectful encounter. Sometimes I want to film somebody, and I ask them for permission, or I'll tell them what I'm doing, and they say, 'No, I don't want to be a part of that', so I just move on. I have to respect when the person doesn't want to be filmed. A lot of my work is predicated on trust, and again, the trust of my subjects, so it's very important that I have that in place before moving forward. It's very rare that I'll film something without the permission of a person.

TH: You said, at some point, that when we look outward we see a reflection of what we first witness inside ourselves – which I guess relates to what you said just now. Could you talk a bit more about that?

KA: Much of my work has to do with showing the audience that there is nothing to fear, showing people that there is nothing to fear. Because a lot of my subjects are on the fringes of society. They're almost what some people would consider 'untouchables', or at the bottom of the societal totem pole, in a sense. And shooting at nighttime in their neighbourhood ... there's not many people that are comfortable even walking through there, even if they live in the local area. My work is really about choosing to see the light in a person instead of the darkness in a person – in the sense of choosing to identify with the love the person has, rather than be afraid of the person.

Perception is a choice; we choose what we see. We look inward first and decide what we want to see and then project it outward onto the world. Focusing on the light in another reinforces it in yourself. And that's why this work, in a sense, is also therapeutic for me. Because it helps to strengthen my attitude about people and life in general, and about the world. I feel like all of us need to change our perception of the world, to some extent. To see it as a safe place, as a loving place, and as a harmless place, but oftentimes we have a past in the world which hasn't been all of those things, and we expect the past to repeat itself. When I'm working, my work is really about healing and letting go of the past and freeing up the future: opening the future up to be free and different from the past.

TH: I think there's something really interesting in what you're saying in relation to affirming or saying, 'I film those people who touch me or who I am drawn to, or who I love and feel connected to and see myself in.' In relation to that, do you see your filming as a form of autobiography?

KA: It was about me to some extent, especially the later half of *IWOW: I Walk on Water* (2020). That dealt more with me, but not me in the autobiographical way; more in my relationships with others. The other people in the film who I'm communicating with – it's about those relationships that we share together. The term 'snapshot' is more appropriate, I feel, because when you take a picture of something, it's never the full truth. There's always stuff that's outside of the frame that isn't picked up in the image.

TH: You said at some point that you see every film you make as a continuation of the previous one or of the next one. Could you talk about this in relation to your process of making and living, how film and life overlap?

KA: My work doesn't exist in a vacuum. I would like people who go and watch *IWOW* ... they don't have to, I feel like the work can stand on itself. *Black Mother* (2018) could stand on its own, *Field Niggas* (2015) could stand on its own, *IWOW* could stand on its own – but as an audience, or as someone who would be coming to my work, there are certain prerequisites, in a sense, that would help you to get more from the films. So if somebody goes to watch *IWOW* after watching *Urban Rashomon* (2010), that would probably help them understand the relationship a lot deeper. I don't always understand who my audience is going to be, and I don't want to judge my audience. I don't judge my subjects and I don't want to judge those who come to view my subjects, either. But, at the same time, I would just love it if people came with an open mind and with an open heart.

My work [is] all a continuation of itself but it may not necessarily be a linear progression. To go from *Black Mother* to *IWOW* ... [they are] different films. I don't want to say completely different, but they're very different [*laughs*]. In subject-matter, I would say *Black Mother* was a personal film in one respect and *IWOW* was a personal film in a whole other respect.

TH: I also was quite interested in this thing you said about not considering your conversations with people as interviews, but testimonies. Why are they testimonies rather than interviews?

KA: Yeah. It's just very casual. I don't tell my subjects what to say. I may open up a conversation where we're both in conversation with each other, or I may ask them direct questions, but it's always in a way that, you know ... they're living a certain life and it's not like how I may be interviewed as an artist in a professional sense and stuff like that. The people who I'm documenting, many of them don't have social media, they're not on Twitter, Tumblr, Instagram, Facebook, any of those things. So, when I come through with the camera – and I've been doing it for years in Harlem, specifically on this corner of 125th and Lexington – I've gained a lot of trust from my subjects, so I value what they offer me. It's almost, in a way, as if they're testifying; they're telling me about their life, their struggle. They're letting me into their hardships.

TH: Maybe one of the reasons why people trust you and feel like talking is because they feel like you're not trying to get something from them. There's not this sense, which you sometimes have with certain kinds of filmmaking, that they're looking for a particular story to tell. Whereas if you feel like someone is listening to your story, but not seeking to get something very particular from you, then perhaps that opens up a different kind of trust and a different kind of feeling of being listened to.

KA: Yeah. I approach my subjects with an open heart and my full trust in them that they'll express what they want to express. I may start off with one or two questions, but they can take it from there. And they can go on to whatever they want to tell me about. I'm there as a listener. And as a filmmaker I feel that that's the best approach to have with the type of documentaries that I make, because I'm writing the film as I'm making it. Through the conversation, through what I'm being told. That becomes the subject-matter, that becomes the structure and the whole substance of the film itself: what people are telling me, you know. If you look at the editing in *IWOW*, you can tell that I didn't edit it in a way to cut people out, to cut out what they're saying. Even if it was something which may have had people looking at me like I exposed myself or I was vulnerable in certain situations.

The number-one thing that I'm looking for in my films is honesty. There's so much fakeness in the world, and there's so much saving face, and people just hiding, and I don't want to do that in my work. One of the reasons why *IWOW* becomes personal, in a sense, is because after all these years of photographing people in a somewhat vulnerable position, such an open position, I felt as if I needed to share my own openness with the world.

TH: Why are you filming on this particular street corner in Harlem, 125th Street and Lexington Avenue, and why at night-time?

KA: 125th Street and New York City/Harlem is the cultural centre of Black awareness in, I would say, the entire United States. You know, you have other pockets of the country that are very conscious, but, historically speaking, 125th has been Mecca. The entire 125th Street. But, you know, as you progress to the eastern part of that street, it's a little bit more run-down, and throughout my life getting knowledge-of-self and focusing on self-education, I spent a lot of time at a school called The Allah School, which is on 7th Avenue and 126th Street, but it's right there, very close to 125th. And I would travel there to study, to go to classes, come up in the 5 per cent nation, you know. But East Harlem, East 125th, is a place I would avoid most of the time because of the heavy police presence, or, you know, you could tell there was a lot of drugs and homelessness in the area. It wasn't until later on that

I began to see that there's stories there. I knew that in order to have access to that it would require dedication. It would require tenacity and courage, and I felt that I had those things and that I wanted to develop that even more myself. I would say that it helped me to grow. It's been a form of maturing, definitely maturing, and learning a lot about people.

Prior to that, I had different jobs which kinda helped me to become a more compassionate person. I worked in nursing homes, two different nursing homes, throughout my adolescence. And that really helped me open my mind up about people who were physically sick, and mentally as well ... Empathy translated into the streets. I grew up between Brooklyn, Queens and Long Island, and at the time that I started that work on 125th and Lex shooting photographs, I had a very comfortable, well-paying job in corporate America, and I was missing the streets, I was missing that, I was missing those earlier impressions of New York City, juxtaposed against this very clean, comfortable job. So, leaving that job at night-time and returning to the streets gave me a sense of reality.

TH: Tell me about Frenchie. How did you meet Frenchie?

KA: Frenchie is somebody who I met in the streets in 2011 at the outset of me becoming a stills photographer. That relationship was predicated on photography. I don't think I would have met Frenchie had I not been a photographer, had I not been stopping people in the streets and taking their portraits. Harlem is a place that we refer to as Mecca, because that's where the knowledge and the wisdom is, and growing up, getting left back in school, going through trials and tribulations, there were certain levels of knowledge that I received through Harlem, because Harlem is a cultural centre, especially for Black people in America. There's all sorts of hidden knowledge and esoteric information that isn't taught in the school system that is extremely important for Black people to learn about themselves, and Harlem afforded me that. Our genesis in Harlem had to do more with the knowledge-of-self. And at that time, I wasn't into art, I wasn't a photographer or a filmmaker. But years later, when I did become a filmmaker and a photographer, I began to focus in on the people that were on the fringes, and Frenchie was one of those people.

So that relationship really goes back to the night of 21 November 2011, when I met Frenchie. I'd taken a portrait of him and came home and developed the film and was thinking that this is somebody who I'd like to continue working with. And for the first six months of working with him – taking pictures of the street at night-time – there wasn't much conversation between us. It was mostly based on photography. It wasn't until maybe six months after meeting him that we actually broke bread and we had a meal together and actually spoke and I got to see that he's coherent and he's actually eloquent and he's full of substance. I made two films in 2013: one was called *Urban Rashomon* and the other was *Antonyms of Beauty*, and both of those films focus heavily on Frenchie and my relationship with him. Frenchie is just someone who I saw the light in, a very bright light, you know what I'm saying? Even though he was in that type of situation with his life, it never hampered his brightness or his inner light.

TH: I also was really drawn to – because I guess it felt quite close to me – something you said about when you were a kid, you would be staring at the sun for hours, even though people told you not to. I thought that was really funny because I've also often been told that I stare too much and there's something interesting in this idea of staring ...

KA: [*laughs*] I still do that. I still do that when I can. I wouldn't say for hours, but for a couple of minutes, for a while. That's nutrition. Your eyes eat light. Your eyes eat and they eat light. You look at certain animals or certain fish that live at the ocean floor. If they don't come up every now and then, they lose their vision. Light is everything. Literally and figuratively. Light is knowledge and everything is light. We become enlightened; it's not something necessarily that we become, it's something we recognise. We recognise our own enlightenment by letting go of the blocks to love that we set up. Because we set up a lot of blocks to love within our relationships, through our grievances, and through our defensiveness. We have to just remain; it's hard to do, especially in this world which is full of attack. There's a strength in defencelessness and laying down your armour and just being open.

What I'm saying now is going a little bit further than what your question was asking, but in short: I love the light, I want to be in the light. That's our natural place. Specifically, just go back to *IWOW*, that film is called *I Walk on Water*. There's a whole segment in that project where I talk about being Christ, and I say I'm Christ, but I never meant and I never mean that I'm Christ alone. I'm Christ as much as you are, Therese. We're all the Christ, we're all the child of God, we're just broken into multiple fragments where we seem to have different names and different personalities. But, relating back to your earlier question about encounter, I'm constantly encountering Christ, I'm constantly encountering the son of God, in all of my subjects. And, you know, to come to identify with that has nothing to do with any denomination or practising any religion or anything like that; it's just a reality that there's divinity in all of us. All of us contain that divinity and that spark of light.

TH: I wonder how it relates to forgiveness, then. You talk also about your films being about forgiveness.

KA: Yeah, well, you know, forgiveness is not necessarily just about being nice or 'I'm such a nice person because I forgive', you know?

Forgiveness is just about being intelligent and letting go of what doesn't have a cause, what has no effects, and what's an illusion. You know, a lot of our grievances are predicated on things that happened in the past, but the past doesn't exist. We constantly renew the past and bring it into the present so that we can maintain those grievances. Forgiveness is just a letting go of those grievances and moving beyond the past and freeing up the future to be something different from the past. So forgiveness is something that is always practised in the now, in the present moment; it's a declaration of freedom to say, I'm not a victim of the past, I'm not a victim of what somebody has done to me, and it's a recognition of your own power: you have the power to forgive.

Forgiveness is the key to happiness. It's really difficult to be happy if you aren't forgiving.

TOWARDS A TRANSPERSONAL 'I'

—

ANNIE ERNAUX

TRANSLATED FROM THE FRENCH
BY DAWN M. CORNELIO

Creating the *history* of my texts seems as risky to me as creating the history of my life. How can I explain an approach whose ins and outs are not clear to me, since each project is the expression of a desire I can't ignore? That being said, I suspect that there is another reason for this reluctance to go back: shining a light on the way in which my books were written is of no use to me for the one I am writing – in front of me, it is still as dark as ever. Can it be useful for others, or some sort of history of writing, this I don't know.

When I started writing *Cleaned Out*, my project was not to uncover all or part of my past life, but just one dimension of it: the transition from a working-class world to a culturally dominant world, thanks to school. I remember that the question of enunciation, *I* or *she*, surfaced immediately. Undecided, I drew lots, and not for the first time. Chance decided it would be *I*, but the fact that I did not try a second time indicates that the dice matched my preference. There was, however, no doubt that the form would be a novel. I would write the story of twenty-year-old Denise Lesur, who, going through an abortion in her university residence, in the 1960s, recalls her childhood and adolescence, up to this event. A very traditional structure. This is how I now analyse this spontaneous, unconscious choice:

* Maintaining doubt about the identity of the *I* with me, the author (even if I was not at all sure of being published, I had to plan for everything). Fiction protects, it is an ambiguous but unassailable position. No one would have the right to say, 'Denise Lesur is you.' I would in fact discover that in an interview it is easier to declare 'Denise holds her parents in contempt' than 'I held my parents in contempt.'
* Enjoying the greatest freedom in writing. The mask of fiction removed all kinds of inner censorship, allowing me to push all the boundaries and expose what remains unspoken about family, sex or school in a violent and derisive way.[1]

* 'Making' literature. At that time, for me, literature was the novel. I needed my personal reality to become literature: only by becoming literature would it become 'true' and something other than an individual experience. I spontaneously used the form which embodied literature in my eyes at that time.

I wrote three books in this belief. I do not question it in the third one, *A Frozen Woman*, since I accept that the word 'novel' appears on the cover, but this time the *I* is anonymous, casting more than a shadow of doubt about it referring to the author. On the other hand, the narrative is constructed through memories, from childhood origins to an indeterminate (because 'frozen') present, which could belong to the author or to the narrator. In short, the uncertain status of this book, evident when I met readers, who often attributed the narrator's experience directly to me and whom I gave up correcting: 'Not me, the heroine.'

Paradoxically, I turned away from the form of the novel with the project of writing about someone other than myself, the project of writing about my father. Not abruptly, in a process that took years (a dozen drafts of a novel, one which reached a hundred pages, attests both to my difficulty in abandoning the genre and my writing blocks), where I questioned writing in general, its role and its meaning as a practice.[2] I came to this conclusion: the only right way to evoke a seemingly insignificant life, my father's, without *betraying* (the social class I came from and which I was going to take as my subject) was to constitute the reality of this particular life and this particular class through precise facts, words heard, the values of the time. The name I gave the project and the manuscript until its completion – the title *A Man's Place*[3] was only set at the very end – clearly reflects my intention: 'Elements towards a family ethnography.' I felt very strongly that the form of the novel was a kind of cheating. To make my father a character, his life a fictional destiny, seemed to me the continued betrayal of life in literature (even if it was no longer a concern of mine to situate myself inside or outside the latter).

Naturally, if *he* referred to a real person, it had to be the same for *I*. Any ambiguity would have robbed the book of its purpose. I included myself in the text as a daughter who shared the same world as my father, a labourer turned shopkeeper, and as a narrator, a professor who had moved into the world of 'legitimate' speech. An in-between space, a real distance that the text exposes, which it is impossible to conceal, because in a book like this the narrator's social and cultural position is essential.

Thus my transition from fictitious *I* to a real *I* is not due to a need to lift the mask but related to a new writing project that I define in *A Woman's Story*[4] as 'something between literature, sociology and history'. By this I mean that I seek to make concrete, by using rigorous means, 'lived' experience, without abandoning what makes the specificity of literature, namely the requirement to write well, the absolute commitment of the subject in the text. It also means, of course, that I reject belonging to a specific genre, be it novel or even autobiography. Autofiction doesn't suit me either. The *I* that I use seems to me an impersonal form, barely gendered, sometimes even a word belonging more to 'the other' than to 'me': a transpersonal form, in short. It's not a way of building an identity for myself, through a text, of autofictionalising myself, but a way of grasping, within my experience, the signs of a family, social or passionate reality. I believe that the two approaches, really, are diametrically opposed.

—

1 Although I wonder if the greatest freedom did not result from the uncertainty about whether or not there would be a publication. When I learned that my manuscript would be published, I was frightened, suddenly aware of what I had written.

2 Private or public events, such as teaching a course on autobiography, played a role in this questioning. In fact, it was almost always life that forced me to revise my writing.
3 Translator's note: this is the title of Tanya Leslie's translation of the novel into English; the source text is simply *La Place*.
4 Translator's note: this is the title of Leslie's translation of the novel into English; the source text is simply *Une Femme*.

FREIGHTED CURRICULUM, AND MY FAMILY AND LANDSCAPE: AN INHERITANCE IN THE FLESH
—
JANE FAWCETT

I film my father's puppies as he and my sister chat about a lady coming to look at a dog with the intention to buy it. You can't see their faces, but my dad starts to talk about the dog smelling – stinking really. So, you can imagine that, and maybe the imagined smell – the stink animates an image of my family. My nephew becomes annoyed with me filming the puppies because he thinks one of them is going to fall off the fence. It is also because he is tired, because he is a child and because he has cancer and at every moment I must take him seriously.

It becomes dramatic. It happens in Wensleydale.

My name is Jane. 'Jane' as in Jane Bowles, Emily Jane Brontë and the girl Jane in the children's books that illustrate what a girl is.

Jane Bowles writes in her diary pretending to be racist because it gives her a methodology. She also writes in her diary about her husband, and how he knows everything about her, including how she is beset by the hatred of her own femininity. He wants her to be happy, but she isn't. He encourages her career in writing, but she doesn't enjoy it. He sends her on a retreat to discourage her moodiness, but she is bored and she gets drunk. She says, 'If possible before I die, I would like to become a little more independent.'

I don't think she means it. I think – she thinks – it's funny. This gives her a methodology too.

Me and Jane and Emmy Moore, her alter ego, the other version of herself.

I cried when I got my GCSE results in English because I got a D. It was the only subject I cared about and thought that without any attempt at trying I was well deserving of an A. There lies in The Wensleydale School, heavy on the curriculum The Brontës, delivered passively and without sentiment by the teachers, ignored by the rest of us because there was also a farm and farm studies and we mostly lived on farms.

I went to Haworth, Brontë Country, with my family on a visit that we made on my birthday at my suggestion. I took loads of photos and listened in to their conversations: it was fertile ground for a clash of internal family cultures and, unbeknown to me, a competition of landscape, labour and weather. This invigorated in my family a smugness; that they went about life with vigour and without complaint. We were in competition with the Brontës, but I knew that we would win because my sister told me that Haworth, Brontë Country, isn't half as rugged as Wensleydale where we're from. My sister returned home satisfied in her certainty that through the cultivation and control of her own landscape, she was stronger.

Before I finish and we all go home there is also another Jane, Jane Doe. She is the placeholder, an unidentified, anonymous and hypothetical average woman and the plaintiff. She is either unknown or she is concealed.

Jane Fawcett was born and spent most of her youth in Wensleydale, North Yorkshire.

DON'T PLAY WITH THAT GIRL

ANDREA LUKA ZIMMERMAN

Sometimes I like to say that I am a filmmaker, because people think it's glamorous, but to explain what kind of film it is that I am making, or what I am seeking, gets complicated, and so occasionally I just sit with the glamorous part and enjoy what it conjures.

'Don't play with that girl,' said his mother, who was completely sure anyone living on that council estate they never entered and wanted to be as far away from as possible – even though they were only down the road, in a house – was a corrupting, or contaminating, influence. True, there exists a newspaper article showing my old housing block with an arrow pointing at it in a large font: 'Working Class Reality', and the newer houses down the road, also with an arrow: 'Middle Class Fantasy'.

I never considered *myself* as 'working class'. We don't until we are forced to, by imposed structural comparison.

I feel a kinship with those who had to hustle to survive; those who learned to hide what happened behind closed doors; those whose bodies were not welcomed by disabling structures, and those who, as kids, received no touch other than violence. I lean towards those who feel shame even after many years of trying to overcome it; those who feel sorrow and confusion as the foundation of their being; who, though they might not always be able to – but always try – want to make a world that is liveable for all, including the non-human; towards those who did not make it.

I used to be a hairdresser. Someone at a bus stop told me about a filmmaking course, and I went there the next day. I didn't have a portfolio; I borrowed one ... To the surprise of my grandmother, who commented, 'You did so well, I was sure you'd become a drug addict.'

However, to make films with the people I do, and when it comes to explaining the process or result to those that ask, and because of the way that culture works and how people are included or excluded from it, it is mostly to people outside that way of living, and although it has now become easier as I can show previous works, I need to do a lot of undoing in response to them telling me, probably with admiration or in support or with some sense of uneasiness, I never can tell, as it appears to them, that I, or rather my work, 'gives voice to the voiceless'. Sometimes, but it happens often enough for me to mention it, I am told that they think that the people in my films 'are so lucky to have met you', that they had 'something creative to do', not thinking that it implies that they assume the people in my work, which is my community, and also me, would otherwise perhaps simply have suffered in misery, as if they had no internal lives of their own. It's peculiar, this, and usually, probably mostly always, entangled with the belief that it is everyone's inevitable desire to move in a certain direction socially, culturally, materially, and so they are part of producing this gaze, not always hostile, of course, but objectifying nonetheless.

So you are out, then you are in, and then, in their way of thinking, you are fine, you are no longer that, move on, get over it. In East Berlin, after Germany's reunification, landlords who filled in and painted over their buildings' bullet-marked facades would receive more funding than those who decided to keep the marks visible. Because there was so little money, the consensus became that pastel was nice.

To maintain a courage for living feels like the hardest, and perhaps *the*, lesson of life. For me, this has been helped by living alongside, and occasionally within, the holding structures of a *chosen* belonging.

My grandfather drank so much that he was never sober but also never appeared drunk anymore. He had been in a Gulag labour camp and then sailed the world; he had butterfly, heart, ship and mermaid tattoos all over his arms and legs, as well as a prison teardrop. Children could still buy alcoholic drinks in shops then, and so he got me to buy the beers as he was banned from most places. When he needed money, he took bets, entering cages where Rottweiler guard dogs were kept. He was never bitten, and I am sure I learned my comfort around dogs from him. His stories always returned to the Gulag. Then I found out he wasn't my mother's real father; I understood the possibilities of what this meant.

We grew up in a relief settlement at the edge of Munich. We were among the first to move in; sheep still ran through the estate. My mother used to cook Spam with tinned mushrooms and rice. Let's just say I retain an ambiguous relationship with the smell of dog food.

I always wore the same clothes and my hair was greasy. 'Don't play with that girl,' I heard them say about me, and add, 'she smells.' I was accustomed to sourcing nourishment in unexpected places. I knew where to look for it, and I was not alone. I still hug trees. I learned to drive a car at thirteen. My friends spoke more languages than I.

'*Don't* pick on that girl,' Sandra would tell him after he continued to bully me, even though it took her, much smaller than me, to show me how to fight back and not simply curl up and cry.

'Don't play with *that* girl,' I was told, but I did, and, when she ran away, I hid her in my wardrobe for nearly a week, until the police came.

'Don't *play* with that girl,' said my mother before her fists rained down on Ramona and me.

My mother had me when she was a child herself. She had been 'given away', as the child of a child refugee with a significant and lasting undiagnosed mental illness.

I used to carry pepper spray then. I remember noticing that the caretaker, whose name I have tried to remember for many years, didn't have that slight bend in the neck that often shows in people who have been in institutions for a long time or who feel beaten down, or who simply rebelled against the order to 'stand up straight'. One evening, when another new boyfriend didn't want me around,

I refused to go home, and the caretaker took me to a drag bar – their girlfriend was performing that evening.

The German language is gendered, and they taught me to speak in a way that would not replicate male dominance. They said it starts with language; that access depends on who is asking; that marginalised spaces are racialised, gendered, disabling; to believe in an otherwise, trusting that dissonance frequently reaches moments of harmony, and to be alert to processes of radical hope. I learned to dream, then; a process of social dreaming.

'Don't play with that *girl*,' said the bouncer about my friend Raoul because he could be a girl less easily than me a boy. Being flat, I had no problem binding and passing, and we went to men-only bars. When Raoul died of AIDS I was not allowed at his funeral because his parents said he wasn't gay, and something broke open in me again.

My first conscious memory is a dream, of being strapped to the back of a lorry, facing the way we'd come, with my parents waving goodbye. I didn't feel sad at all. Then the lorry and I joined a circus, and it became wild.

Even before primary school, I started hearing people say I seemed different. Later I heard that I seemed weird. I felt uneasy about it. Especially since, even now, I sometimes stare at people, looking for something, forgetting they can see me, too.

For a long time, I feared that I was what others perceived me to be. And as, often, that perception was that I was peculiar, this became a self-fulfilling dilemma. Over time I learned not to worry about it, to understand that I am drawn to those who move their mouths, hands, limbs in ways un/familiar to me. It stirs something, a sense of possibility, almost like when someone whom one has barely noticed suddenly says something completely unexpected, which then changes how you see that person, probably forever, and suddenly you have all the time in the world for them. Or they for you.

*

Exclusion is the rule in binary practice (either/or), whereas poetics aims for the space of difference – not exclusion but, rather, where difference is realized in going beyond.
— Édouard Glissant

The way I make films is by wanting to see something that *is* there but which is often *unseen* owing to persistent cultural tropes, such as the ways in which my and others' pasts are so often represented as only realist, abject, in need of charitable support – that perpetuates a way of being visible based on erasure, a kind of plastering over, like the pastel colours of the 'new' Berlin. The critical thinker, writer and artist Morgan Quaintance calls this experience a 'marginal melancholy', where structures demand an ongoing performance of lack.

Shame. Structures and practices based on extraction and domination, that marginalise because they simply do, because they can and, mainly, because to own the imagination is power. Power is slippery; we often only notice it when it is enacted on (our) bodies.

In *Unexamined Life* (dir. Astra Taylor, 2008), philosopher Judith Butler and artist and disability activist Sunaura Taylor talk about how bodies are not just agents of resistance but also fundamentally in need of support. Official narratives delegate pity towards vulnerability, in turn contributing to the disabling. Because film is foremost a visual art, you must ask, what do you see? How do you see?

Poet and essayist Eileen Myles speaks about this in another way, one I feel close to in my own way of working, a 'seeing *with*' those that will be there once the work is finished, and this knowing becoming part of the making. The invitation into it.

And my whole way of doing this therefore is laden with the ambition for the product to have a lot of world in it, be a little humble, messy and dirty, so that people can enter like they walk into a building, a public building that is there since once I am done it's theirs. I vanish into it first but then you do too. I guess it's 'my writing' but really it's a common practice. That's my dream.[1]

At the same time, for the critical geographer Doreen Massey this seeing takes place in *space*, which is a social dimension. When we are able to look at what is present in a place all at once, we quite literally see different time zones at work: generations, values, experiences and communities all brushing, blurring, merging and shifting with and against each other, to produce a feeling, a history of space that is multifarious. And importantly, for Massey, space initially offers a moment of respect. Time, then, in space, allows for the emergence of relations, a process of relations.

There's a looking at each other, a possibility of seeing, which is something that we can feel when it happens. In this way of thinking, space is the dimension of radical simultaneity: a convivium of stories, the possibility of coexistence. Time is the dimension of sequence, of what is before, now and to come. Historians of 'progress' turn space into a sequence. They claim as an unequivocal positive all that is brand new, vibrant, so-called lively and diverse, convenient, better, modern and safe. What this implies is that all that is not new, is old. That what is not now vibrant, lively and diverse is inconvenient, outdated, impoverished, unsafe or risky. In this vision the future's history is already fixed, it is laid out towards what is deemed inevitable, without deviation towards 'modernisation', such as the need to raise rents or the need to demolish.

This narrative of inevitability masks the conditions by which we end up in this dilemma in the first place, be it through laws, policy, the perverse power of corporations or the machinery of marginalisation, derogating everything that does not fit this narrative of progress. Those who do not fit into these new worlds – those who are less wealthy, socially disadvantaged people, disabled people, drifters, animals, anyone who lives a life that is not part of these ideas – are the ones to be narrativised as marginal. For Massey, difference is reduced to a place in the historical queue, whether that means the working class, the global majority or all those who have not yet arrived in the promised land where, according to the law of capital, we should all be actively headed.

This is what interests me: this movement, which is very subtle, of perception, is a shift *in* perception.

For instance, the privatised city, or one that proposes a privatised space – which includes militarised private cars, private healthcare, private everything – has its mirror image in the Other, producing clichés and stereotypes that reinforce the abject and public fear, and which then marginalise even further by making people feel unwelcome, and in fact, in time, they're not welcome to participate at all, becoming undesired strangers in their own time and place.

Many more of us are not from an inheritance class than are. Many more of us are not the ones who've never had to work, or who've never had to walk because they could afford a bus ticket, or who've never had to take a bus because they have other means of transport, are proliferators of corporate greed and ecologically disastrous pension schemes, property developers, buy-to-let landlords, private school proponents, insurance schemers ...

For most of my life I lived on different versions of so-called 'sink' estates. I lived on the last one for eighteen years, and because of the stability it offered I was able to start a journey of healing.

'Don't play with that girl,' he would say, and mean Sammy, who reminded me of when I was her age, where everything was for the taking, including my bike, which I eventually got back. Later, before he became housebound, Jeff burned down the sorry remnants of a playground, and this became our bonfire pit. He turned one of the frequently burned and long-abandoned cars on the estate into a cat car, and another into a fox car, where we put scraps of food. Another neighbour, John, cut off the tips of his shoes to make sandals, not because he couldn't afford new shoes, he said, but because he didn't need two pairs, so why not be creative?

I started the *Estate* project because of all of this. Jeff refused to leave his flat and his two little dogs because the public retirement homes won't allow pets. I've never understood why this is so, and why meals on wheels are being distributed by delivery robots instead of people, or why the post office had to be privatised because it made 'only' £50 million profit. Jeff was sure they wanted him to die to avoid the need to rehouse him. He was always in pain. He said: 'I've got a little dog here, and my little dog has got more sense than all the governments have ever had. They're nothing but a load of thieves. Oh, they are! They're thieves. They're the ones that get away with those big crimes, and the money. They're the ones. And if we do a small offence – like we diddle a bit of money out of social security – they come down on us like a tonne of bricks, and yet they can take millions. They can take millions ... and they do. And they do.'

I felt at home there, whatever I looked like, often not wanting to speak then, wanting to speak, having to listen. I learned to listen. I knew a door would always be open, and mine was too. I learned how to look out for others as part of a community, in and of difference. The place simply didn't conform to the processes of gentrification. And my films draw on this idea of obstinacy and creative waywardness, instead of simply resilience, towards lives more fluid than finance and power and property want to allow.

The film's frame cannot contain everything that it tries to hold, so there is a necessary messiness to that holding, a layering. I seek a cinematic vernacular, one of fragments, of imperfect memory, glimpses, unpredictable encounters; to start way down the road of a 'story', not to plod through the tired cause-and-effect or beginning, transformation and end. Who gets to tell what story, and how to tell it ...

The film 'industry' demands assimilation towards an expression that is deemed 'cinematic' by the gatekeepers of funding bodies. There is seldom any genuine desire for expression in ways that may yet not be quite understood; for those who think through and with, not about. Our lives are not reducible to just one way of feeling, saying, seeing, telling.

In making *Estate, a Reverie* (2015), we initiated a housing campaign that became visible because we installed a large-scale public artwork called *i am here* (2009–14) on the facade of our building. The work was featured on the BBC, in magazines and newspapers; it received a lot of attention. I tried so hard to find a producer who wanted to help this film, and when I did, the famous producer said, 'You have to use a three-act structure: this is our struggle, this is how we struggled, and this is what happened.' Our film needed reducing, in his mind, to a schema of the same kind that produces the very conditions of our undoing, socially and economically. We know that there is no one story, so why insist on one form to tell them all?

In *And Our Faces, My Heart, Brief as Photos* (1984), writer and storyteller John Berger wrote: 'There is no word in any traditional European language which does not either denigrate or patronise the urban poor in its naming. That is power.' I met Berger in 2012, and he read passages from his novel *King* (1999) for my film *Taskafa, Stories of the Street* (2013): 'A mistake, King, is hated more than an enemy. Mistakes don't surrender as enemies do. There is no such thing as a defeated mistake. Mistakes either exist or they don't. And if they do, they have to be covered over. And we are their mistake, King. Never forget that.'

The book ends with a dream of survival, with King the dog feverish, running for sheer life towards refuge, for collective survival, reaching the wide opening of a beach, the sea ahead, the sounds of the bulldozers and police cars drowned out by the waves, and yet, upon turning around, King sees that there is no one else left. It was a fever dream. It is a daring dream to think otherwise.

My work features animals, often dogs, as they occupy a peculiar and particular place in our human history. They see us for who we are, rather than as a number or as 'other'. They will recognise us. To me, urban animals are witnesses in the face of power: the power we grant them, and how we appropriate them. Hope, here, is always the process of finding beauty, especially in those places deemed ugly, pathetic, insignificant. The pathetic as a refusal of the gaze of power is an idea I heard Eileen Myles speak about. This is a beautiful idea.

I will likely always feel drawn to, or most at ease, in less regulated places. I am drawn in my making to lives lived at the edges, even if – and perhaps especially when – those lives are first glimpsed, often in the public eye, visible but not seen. I don't believe the idea of 'overcoming' one's situation is helpful, as it implies there is an end to something. If this were true (that we can arrive, instead of seeing life as a daily practice of doing and undoing), we would not continue to have the kind of fatal injustices we do.

Filmmaking to me is not confessional but shared and contested, troubled and alive. Sometimes stories, even poetic or lyrical ones, need context and sometimes they don't. I am drawn to bodies that can show us what they carry; words are often not enough. And sometimes images too are not enough to reveal a feeling: some things cannot be shown.

We can lean on others but not so much as to make them tumble over. Similarly, when someone leans on us, we need to take care not to let them tumble when we step aside. Of course, at times in intimate relations and friendships this kind of over-leaning may be necessary, and possible. I believe, too, that sometimes we need to hear our stories told by someone else, as this might allow us to take the space, too. This is how I learned to speak, and this is a process I learned from Forum Theatre, and especially from the rehearsals during the making of *Here for Life* (2019).

In 1985, in an interview for the BBC's *Arena*, writer Jean Genet said, 'I enjoyed making a clumsy kind of theatre. And by being clumsy, perhaps there was something new about it.' How does one find this clumsy stranger within oneself, the creative person who isn't constantly self-censoring? We know that we see what we know. With each new film there is a need to see in a way that we don't yet know. To see *together*, because of the entanglement of all our lives (in the fullest meaning, beyond the human-centric, the thin spaces), and so to encounter both the other in front of us and the stranger within.

There are many contradictions; the world I am drawn to is incomplete. I watch a lot of films that are technically accomplished but which are unfinished, because they never went on the journey that mattered with the people they filmed. Properly thinking through our lives is precious and fragile.

So that's how I think of my approach, which I hope is far from the extractive, industrial and normalising.

Before I made my first long film, in order to make the work on a certain scale I learned that we needed deeply to collaborate; in that way, we can enable each other to act tenfold instead of just doubling. At the turn of the century, I co-founded Vision Machine Film Project with Christine Cynn, Joshua Oppenheimer and Michael Uwemedimo. We explored how to make films with people as a practice of self-(re)imagining. In the early 2000s we offered a free film school for local people in the East End of London and worked in the United States and Indonesia to track the aftermath of state-sanctioned violence and the production of ideology and myth though mainstream cinema as a way to deny the foregrounding of secreted[2] historical and contemporaneous, murderous forms of injustice.

To be creative in the face of power; to know that suffering manifests differently, and often circumstantially, and never to forget to strive to make a space for those less able to participate (and to know how fragile that space is); to make space inside oneself for what one does not know and may never know, but still to know it is real and not to paint that space over.

As where I live (Hackney, London, in social housing) has changed, so also has my need to hide my postcode to get a job. I live on the 'poor door' staircase of my block, something I campaigned against for so long. And yet now, being here, I am grateful for it – that my neighbours are not the millionaires living next door, that they do not engage lawyers to force you to take your chattering parrot indoors so they can 'work' (as happened to a friend nearby); to live in a way where we have to negotiate our communal space, even when there are problems, as a coming together, attempting to figure out some of the various, often gloriously incompatible ways of expressing what it is to be alive. Where you find the courage aged 85 or 92 to squat outside the housing office in a caravan because they say you have a minimum five-year wait until you qualify for housing. And where this doesn't go unnoticed.

---

1 Eileen Myles, *For Now* (New Haven, CT, and London: Yale University Press, 2020), p. 73.

2 I developed this idea of secreting history in 'Secreting History: Spectral and Spectacular Representations of Political Violence' (PhD thesis, 2006), an extract of which appeared in Andrea Luka Zimmerman, 'Secreting History – Screening "History"': 21 Takes', *La Furia Umana*, 36, 2019, www.lafuriaumana.it/index.php/69-archive/lfu-36/888-andrea-luka-zimmerman-secreting-history-screening-history-21-takes, and culminated in the feature documentary *Erase and Forget* (2017).

PEPE PEPE PEPE
—
UMAMA HAMIDO

It's difficult to write about my film and the politics behind it while still making it. I started filming with my friend Mohammad in the summer of 2018, and continued until December 2021. It took place in and around Stratford Shopping Centre, where many homeless people were staying at night. I am now exploring the sound recordings I made during that time (more than 40 hours' worth), listening for hours and hours while transcribing selected sections. Being on the ground and behind the camera, being present in the event itself, is so different from watching and listening to it in front of a screen. A distance has been formed by then, between the I and the subject, and one transitions from a participant to a witness and an observer. Though one never stops being one – it's just that retreating from the event changes our position and perspective on it. It was difficult to go through this transition at first, but soon after, the listening process became a whole new world; it's as if you are entering deeper and deeper into your subject. It's a meditation in itself. Some of the following text is extracted from real dialogues between Mohammad and me; other parts of the text are from my diary.

I developed some kind of obsession in wanting to portray everything, the stories of the streets, the encounters, the people, the details of life, the struggle for survival and the killing of time, the joy of emptiness. What am I talking about? Who are these people and where did they all come from? How did they end up being there? And Mohammad and me? Repetition, that's what addiction is all about? Addicted to the loop, to the feelings, to the thoughts, to the smells, and to a certain melancholia, nothing makes sense but somehow it all rhymes.

On the stairs of the Old Town Hall, Stratford, London
11pm, 3 February 2019
U: So you witness Pepe dying?
M: No no, Pepe was with me like me and you now.
U: You try to save him?
M: He ask me for £4 to buy marijuana. He had £6 on him. A hundred per cent, I have it, but I am thinking I need to keep it to buy breakfast. That's what I think. I tell him no, you see night-time Pepe? Around 11? You have population of friends, they will help you. So I go sit down, one of my friends come and tell me let's go to Westfield, chill next to the cinema. So I get up and follow him. Pepe end up buying spice, and when he take the spice and mix it with the cig the fuckin Asian gave him, he mix it up and smoke it, then get up and ask all homeless on the floor who wants to smoke. Everybody said no, he go and sit down again, he smoke smoke smoke, that's it, finish.
U: Did you try to save him?
M: You know how I try? I come from Westfield, I go to Stratford Centre, I see one of Pepe's best friends, a woman. She come and tell me Mohammad Mohammad come and see what's wrong with Pepe. I said what's wrong. She said the hand is blue, the lips are blue, everywhere is blue. You know white people when you die, your body is blue innit? So I am thinking to myself, what's the meaning of this blue? I remember some movies, and it's there I see the dead

body where the hand is blue, and lips is blue, I understand, I run, I tell her let's go. So we go see Pepe. You know when Pepe is drunk, he sleeps. It doesn't matter what time. I come I see him lying on the floor. I hold his leg Pepe Pepe Pepe. Nothing happen, no move no breath no sound. So after I tell the girl, call paramedics. They tell her what we have to do and we do it. After they come. For 40 min they're checking Pepe. After too much police officer come too, but paramedics get up and go. I ask police officer, why paramedics don't take this body. Police tell me he's dead. Then he tell all homeless in Stratford Centre get out and sleep outside on the street. But there's another car come and pick the body. Pepe was amazing. You know Rasta? If Rasta give Pepe food, Pepe always give me the food. He come and ask me Mohammad do you want food? I said yes.
He give me the food.
U: Where was he from?
M: South Africa, you know. Mix race, amazing, everybody know him.
U: Everybody was sad?
M: Yes, everybody shock. You know Stratford Centre after we wake up? He go to the park, where the basketball is, that's where they hang around during the day.
U: How old was he?
M: I don't know, maybe 50, maybe 40 because he look young, he got baby face, but he's mix race. Mother is rich, father is rich, they live in London. Mother tell Pepe come back home. Pepe said no, I love the street. He tell me this.
U: Because it's the community he's after, and the drugs.
M: If my mother tell me this, I am going home 100%.
U: But you don't go home because you can't.
M: Going home will help me move away from alcoholic life, from everything, you understand?
U: Your home is far, far away like mine.
M: Soon, inshallah, everything can take long.

From my diary
20 December 2021
A full stop to everything. How come and how can that even be possible? Silence. Sounds harsh after all the noise and the traffic and the voices and the never-ending adventures and the nights and the days and the habits formed along the way, addictions and intensity of time and space. Can someone quit a life? Or what kind of life would someone want to quit? Quitting the quitting. Even quitting the idea of quitting, and the repetition, painful and addictive at the same time, highly recommended so that one might wonder how and where they can run away with all these thoughts and definitions. Defining oneself, finding space and solitude among crowded souls and poisoned wind. A fresh start, a restart, can that even be possible?

On the stairs of the Old Town Hall, Stratford, London
10pm, 8 October 2019
M: I am happy you come visit me you know. I like it, you know why?
U: Why?
M: Because I need your company.
U: Even me. Because when I come hang out on the streets I always learn something, it keeps me grounded and slows time down, you know why? Because London is very fast. Look how people move. But now it's corona, it's different, but still harsh. When I sit here I can see life, you know, I feel home, people always want something from each other all the time, calculating, and money and things, they will never love you for only who you are, we sit and just chat, we be, you know, we just chill together, watch, and listen.
M: And enjoy the weather you know, see the trees, the grass, the floor, the birds, it's a miracle. I love this world, I don't say I love London, but I say I love the whole world, because it's only one moon, one sun, not this country have sun and that has another. Boy Allah is

amazing, if Allah can calculate everything in this world the way it is, that's something else.
U: Who are we?
M: We angels
U: Look at the sky.

M: Ya, you know angels? It's we. Because every human being Allah said no problem, you can talk. But not the animals. Not the seafood, not the birds, not the insects, they don't talk.
U: Yes they do, they just have a different language.
M: For themselves. If they talk it's too much complaints. Flies will come when something is broken. And you don't remember ... All what you see is signs, if the bird come is a sign, so we calculate the signs, why they're here. You want food? I go to the shop I buy food give you, no problem.
U: I wish I have socks, you know, that's why I am cold.
M: Me I love the weather, it's nice.

From my diary
10 March 2021
Pitch black, cigarette butts on the floor, torn papers, pens of all colours, plastic bags full of rotten food, and so many details that are tiring to the eye. Nasty smell in the room. Mohammad lies down on his bed. He had lost lots of weight. I came closer, I sat on the bed and felt it was wet. It's Mohammad's sweat. How long has he been lying down here? He woke up and said something I couldn't understand. Why did you come here? And how did they let you in here in the hostel? Ah it's because I am sick! I don't remember since when I have been sleeping, you see.

Look it's the big speaker standing by the wall. You still have it? Yes. Remember the time you used to drag it behind you all the time and take it everywhere. It slept next to you on the floor. You used to tie it to your foot, so that if thieves decide to steal it at night, they will have to untie it from under the red and white sleeping bag that you used to cover your body with. Remember? You had so much energy and you were always very excited. That's why you had to carry it all the time. You want me to play you music? Reggae but not Bob Marley? Ok you think Bob Marley is rubbish now. Fine.

Where's the boat? Let's go to the boat? Why do you want to go to the boat? It's there where we're going to find crack. You know that I stopped everything, all the bad habits. I don't like smoking tobacco anymore. It doesn't come to my mind. Weed, never again. Cider no way. That's it, finish. Done with all these things. But crack, man! When I smoke it I stop coughing, it removes the cough and all the pain in my brain. I forgot where I parked my boat? I have 27 boats. Minus two that I gave to my brother. Minus two that I gave to Marios. Minus two that I lost. How many are left? Come on calculate. Use your fingers and calculate! I am rich. Very very rich. Of course you are. Right now I can buy anything. You know the other day I opened a letter and it was from the Home Office. They wrote to me. They said Pa Mohammad Gaye, you got the Leave to Remain. Is that possible? Isn't my lawyer supposed to receive the letters on my behalf? Or maybe this is a special occasion and they need to communicate directly with me? They really have a very good heart and are very generous. God bless them and bless the mothers who granted such seeds to the world.

In Mohammad's room in a hostel in East London
10 March 2021
M: The moon is out daytime man. The sun is out daytime, but when it's night-time the stars are out. Those stars mean something.

A Toods And Keys... 1 World
Smiling coves up all problems and
solve mean problems... 1 CULTURE
People with respect and under...
standing come with best civic 1st right ideas

Silenc remove you from unnecssary
aracument...
Mobile phone have sound and Silenc...
Hate luck all the doors and
can't open the doors again

U: Yes.

M: There are some human being on earth here they are so important in a way that, each human being, you are one of the stars.

M: Every time, every night around 10, 11, 12, whole way up to tomorrow morning I play Quran, translated in English, I put the volume up too much. These things that always keep knocking, they never knock again. Now when I am not listening to Quran I can still hear it. I read my books I draw draw draw, this is why I draw, because of stress I have which you don't understand this kind of stress, every human being you know yourself. You know what you've been through, everything. Even how you did it, or where, your feelings and your mind, you know why. Living in that office made me draw every type of picture you saw, 100%, and I don't draw again, because I don't have stress, I have headache. It's headache I don't know what headache is this. Human being you have to figure it out yourself, not people figure out it for you, means these people they don't know themselves. Me I know so I take my time to meditate.

M: All the homeless life I been through all ...
U: Too much.
M: My tears drop for it. Me I see too much. Me I don't want no human being to advice me nothing, every 24 hours it's not important at all. That's why I go angry. I don't have time for these things.

M: You don't see the artwork I do in this building, all is five finger. A3 paper I design some amazing pic which ... I don't have even money. But when I have I go photocopy 60. You know how I gonna share this 60, because this is the street ... This is the highway this is the main road for Lincoln Road ...

All my artwork ... and the rest I give it away there. I draw 35 pic which I give for free, but before I give for free I photocopy 300 400 900 copies.

—
Drawings by Mohammad Gaye

OTHER THAN MYSELF/ MY OTHER SELF
—
TRINH T. MINH-HA

Every voyage can be said to involve a re-siting of boundaries. The travelling self is here both the self that moves physically from one place to another, following 'public routes and beaten tracks' within a mapped movement; and the self that embarks on an undetermined journeying practice, having constantly to negotiate between home and abroad, native culture and adopted culture, or, more creatively speaking, between a here, a there *and* an elsewhere.

Travelling Tales

A public place around a train station. In Marrakech. In Fez. In a city of words, told by a husky voice. In a body full of sentences, proverbs, and noises. There, a story is born. This body is a fountain. Water is an image. The source travels. A crowd of children and women wait in line in front of the well. Water is scarce. Stories heap up at the bottom of the well...

These images land in disorder. They reach me from afar and speak to me in my mother tongue, an Arabic dialect riddled with symbols. This language, which one speaks but does not write, is the warm fabric of my memory. It shelters and nourishes me.

Can it withstand the travel, the shifts, the extreme mobility in the new clothes of an old foreign language? Out of modesty, it retains its secrets and only rarely does it give itself in. It is not it that travels. It is I who carry a few fragments of it.[1]

The source moves about; it travels. Tahar Ben Jelloun's fountain-body unfolds through movements of words, images of water, sensations of mother-memory, and sounds of travelling fictions.

These come in disorder, he wrote, doubting that Mother's language at home – or Language – will ever be able to withstand the mobility of the journey. Never quite giving itself in, however, Language remains this inexhaustible reservoir from which noises, proverbs and stories continue to flow when water is scarce. Thus, it is not 'It' that travels. It is 'I' who carries here and there a few fragments of It. In this cascade of words, where and which is the source finally? I or It? For memory and language are places both of sameness and otherness, dwelling and travelling. Here, Language is the site of return, the warm fabric of a memory, and the insisting call from afar, back home. But here also, there, and everywhere, language is a site of change, an ever-shifting ground. It is constituted, to borrow a wise man's words, as an 'infinitely interfertile family of species spreading or mysteriously declining over time, shamelessly and endlessly hybridizing, changing its own rules as it goes'.[2]

It is often said that writers of colour, including anglophone and francophone Third World writers of the diaspora, are condemned to write only autobiographical works. Living in a double exile – far from the native land and far from their mother tongue – they are thought to write by memory and to depend to a large extent on hearsay. Directing their look towards a long bygone reality, they supposedly excel in reanimating the ashes of childhood and of the country of origin. The autobiography can thus be said to be an abode in which the writers mentioned necessarily take refuge. But to preserve this abode, they would have to open it up and pass it on. For not every detail of their individual lives bears recounting in such an 'autobiography', and what they choose to recount no longer belongs to them as individuals. Writing from a representative space that is always politically marked (as 'coloured' or as 'Third World'), they do not so much remember for themselves as they remember in order to tell. When they open the doors of the abode and step out of it, they have, in a sense, freed themselves again from 'home'. They become a passage, start the travel anew, and pull themselves at once closer and further away from it by telling stories.

A shameless hybrid: I or It? Speaker or Language? Is it Language which produces me, or I who produce language? In other words, when is the source 'here' and when is it 'there'? Rather than merely enclosing the above writers in a place recollected from the past, the autobiographical abode propels them forward to places of the present – foreign territories, or the lands of their adopted words and images. 'The writer writes so that he no longer has a face', T. B. Jelloun remarked. 'One relapses into memory as one relapses into childhood, with defeat and damage. Even if it were only to prevent such a fall, the writer sees to it that he is in a layer of "future memory", where he lifts and displaces the stones of time.'[3] Journeying across generations and cultures, tale-telling excels in its powers of adaptation and germination; while with exile and migration, travelling expanded in time and space becomes dizzyingly complex in its repercussive effects. Both are subject to the hazards of displacement, interaction and translation. Both, however, have the potential to widen the horizon of one's imagination and to shift the frontiers of reality and fantasy, or of Here and There. Both contribute to questioning the limits set on what is known as 'common' and 'ordinary' in daily existence, offering thereby the possibility of an elsewhere-within-here, or -there.

An African proverb says, 'A thing is always itself and more than itself.' Tale-telling brings the impossible within reach. With it, I am who It is, whom I am seen to be, yet I can only feel myself there where I am not, vis-à-vis an elsewhere I do not dwell in. The tale, which belongs to all countries, is a site where the extraordinary takes shape from the reality of daily life. Of all literary genres, it is the one to circulate the most, and its extreme mobility has been valued both for its local specificity and for its capacity to speak across cultural and ethnic boundaries. To depart from one's own language of origin, to be able to acknowledge that 'the source moves about', to fare like a foreigner in this language, and to return to it via its travelling fragments is also to learn how to be silent and to speak again, differently. T. B. Jelloun opens, for example, his well-known tale of *Moha the Fool, Moha the Sage* (*Moha le fou, Moha le sage*) with an epigraph which reminds the reader of the political death of a man and goes on to affirm: 'It doesn't matter what the official declarations say. A man has been tortured. To resist the pain, to overcome the suffering, he resorted to a strategy: to recollect the most beautiful remembrances of his short life.'[4] And on this statement unfolds the telling of the man, as captured and transmitted by Moha, or as written by Jelloun himself.

A Stranger in a Strange Country

'He's a stranger,' Louise said joyfully. 'I always thought so – he'll never really fit in here.'
'How long are you going to keep me prisoner?' he asked.
'Prisoner?' answered the director, frowning. 'Why do you say prisoner? The Home isn't a jail. You weren't allowed to go out for several days for reasons of hygiene, but now you're free to go wherever you like in the city.'
'Excuse me,' said Akim, 'I meant to say: when can I leave the Home?'
'Later,' said the director, annoyed, 'later. And besides, Alexander Akim, that depends on you. When you no longer feel like a stranger, then there will be no problem in becoming a stranger again.'[5]

Much has been written on the achievements of exile as an artistic vocation, but as a travelling voice from Palestine puts it, exile on the twentieth-century scale and in the present age of mass immigration, refugeeism and displacement 'is neither aesthetically nor humanistically comprehensible'. This 'irremediably secular and unbearably historical' phenomenon of untimely massive wandering remains 'strangely compelling to think about but terrible to experience' (Edward Said).[6] For people who have been dispossessed and forced to leave for an uncertain destiny, rejected time and again, returned to the sea or to the no man's land of border zones; for these unwanted expatriated, it seems that all attempts at exalting the achievements of exile are but desperate efforts to quell the crippling sorrow of homelessness and estrangement. The process of rehabilitation which involves the search for a new home appears to be above all a process by which people stunned, traumatised and mutilated by the shifts of event that have expelled them from their homelands learn to adjust to their sudden state of isolation and uprootedness.

Refugeeism, for example, may be said to be produced by political and economic conditions that make continued residence intolerable. The irreversible sense of 'losing ground' and losing contact is, however, often suppressed by the immediate urge to 'settle in' or to assimilate in order to overcome the humiliation of bearing the too-many-too-needy status of the homeless-stateless alien. The problem that prevails then is to be accepted rather than to accept. 'We are grateful. We do not want to be a nuisance', said a Vietnamese male refugee in Australia who, while feeling indebted to his host country, believes that only in Vietnam can a Vietnamese live happily.[7] Or else, 'We are a disturbance. That's the word. Because we show you in a terrible way how fragile the world we live in is ... You didn't know this in your skin, in your life, in every second of your life', said a less grateful Cambodian woman refugee in France who considers Paris to be, in the racial distances it maintains, 'a city of loneliness and ghosts'.[8] Intensely connected with the history and the politics that have erupted to displace them, refugees are unwanted persons whose story has been an embarrassment for

everyone, as it 'exposes power politics in its most primitive form
... the ruthlessness of major powers, the brutality of nation-states,
the avarice and prejudice of people.'[9] Dispossessed not only of their
material belongings but also of their social heritages, refugees lead
a provisional life, drifting from camps to camps, disturbing local
people's habits and destabilising the latter's lifestyle when they move
into a neighbourhood. However they are relocated, they are a burden
on the community. On the one hand, migrant settlements can turn
out to be 'centers of hopelessness' which soon become 'centers of
discontent'. On the other hand, those who succeed in resettling are
blamed for usurping the work from someone else, and those who
fail to secure happiness in their adopted lands are accused of being
ungrateful, worsening thereby a situation in which exclusionary
policies have been advocated on the ground that the rich host nations
will soon be put in 'the poorhouse' by the flood of refugees – because
'they multiply'.[10]

    Great generosity and extreme gratitude within sharp hostility;
profound disturbance for both newcomers and old-timers: the
experience of exile is never simply binary. If it's hard to be a
stranger, it is even more so to stop being one. 'Exile is neither
psychological nor ontological', wrote Maurice Blanchot. 'The exile
cannot accommodate himself to his condition, nor to renouncing
it, nor to turning exile into a mode of residence. The immigrant is
tempted to naturalize himself, through marriage for example, but
he continues to be a migrant.'[11] The one named 'stranger' will never
really fit in, so it is said, joyfully. To be named and classified is to
gain better acceptance, even when it is a question of fitting in a
no-fit-in category. The feeling of imprisonment denotes here a mere
subjection to strangeness as confinement. But the Home, as it is
repeatedly reminded, is not a jail. It is a place where one is compelled
to find stability and happiness. One is made to understand that if one
has been temporarily kept within specific boundaries, it is mainly for

one's own good. Foreignness is acceptable once I no longer draw the line between the others and myself. First assimilate, and then be different within permitted boundaries. 'When you no longer feel like a stranger, then there will be no problem in becoming a stranger again.' As you come to love your new home, it is thus implied, you will immediately be sent back to your old home (the authorised and pre-marked ethnic, gender or sexual identity), where you are bound to undergo again another form of estrangement. Or else, if such a statement is to be read in its enabling potential, then, unlearning strangeness as confinement becomes a way of assuming anew the predicament of deterritorialisation: it is both I and It that travel; the home is here, there, wherever one is led to in one's movement.

Wanderers across Language

> Our present age is one of exile. How can one avoid sinking into the mire of common sense, if not by becoming a stranger to one's own country, language, sex and identity? Writing is impossible without some kind of exile. Exile is already in itself a form of *dissidence* ... a way of surviving in the face of the *dead father* ... A woman is trapped within the frontiers of her body and even of her species, and consequently always feels *exiled* both by the general clichés that make up a common consensus and by the very powers of generalization intrinsic to language. This female in exile in relation to the General and to Meaning is such that a woman is always singular, to the point where she comes to represent the singularity of the singular – the fragmentation, the drive, the unnameable.[12]

Perhaps, 'a person of the twentieth century can exist honestly only as a foreigner',[13] suggests Julia Kristeva. Supposedly a haven for

the persecuted and the homeless, Paris, which has offered itself
to many stateless wanderers as a second home ever since the late
nineteenth century, is itself a city whose houses, as Walter Benjamin
described them, 'do not seem made to be lived in, but are like stones
set for people to walk between'.[14] The city owes its liveliness to the
movements of life that unfold in the streets. Here, by choice or by
necessity, pedestrians, passers-by, visitors, people in transit can all
be said to 'dwell' in passageways, strolling through them, spending
their time and carrying on most of their activities outside the
houses, in the intervals of the stonework. Such a view of Paris
would contribute to offsetting the notion of home and dwelling as
a place and a practice of fixation and sameness. For after all, where
does dwelling stop? In a built environment where outside walls
line the streets like inside walls, and where the homey enclosures
are so walled off, so protected against the outside that they appear
paradoxically set only 'for people to walk between', outsiders have
merely brought with them one form of outsideness: that very form
others who call themselves insiders do not – out of habit – recognise
as their own insideness.

'Modern Western culture', remarks Said, 'is in large part the
work of exiles, émigrés, refugees.'[15] If it seems obvious that the
history of migration is one of instability, fluctuation and discontinuity,
it seems also clear for many Third World members of the diaspora
that their sense of group solidarity, of ethnic and national identity,
has been nourished in the milieus of the immigrant, the refugee and
the exiled. Here, identity is a product of articulation. It lies at the
intersection of dwelling and travelling and is a claim of continuity
within discontinuity (and vice versa). A politics rather than an inherited
marking, its articulation and re-articulation grows out of the very
tension raised between these two constructs – one based on
socio-cultural determinants and the other, on biological ones.
The need to revive a language and a culture (or to reconstitute a

nation out of exile, as in the case of the Palestinian struggle) thus develops *with* the radical refusal to indulge in exile as a redemptive motif, and to feel uncritically 'at home in one's own home', whether this home is over there or over here. Such a stance goes far beyond any simplistic positive assertions of ethnic or sexual identity, and it is in this difficult context of investigation of self that, rather than constituting a privilege, exile and other forms of migration can become 'an *alternative* to the mass institutions that dominate modern life'.[16]

Home and language tend to be taken for granted; like Mother or Woman, they are often naturalised and homogenised. The source becomes then an illusory secure and fixed place, invoked as a natural state of things untainted by any process or outside influence (by 'theory', for example), or else as an indisputable point of reference whose authority one can unfailingly rely on. Yet language can only live on and renew itself by hybridising shamelessly and changing its own rules as it migrates in time and space. Home for the exile and the migrant can hardly be more than a transitional or circumstantial place, since the 'original' home neither can be recaptured nor can its presence/absence be entirely banished in the 'remade' home. Thus, figuratively but also literally speaking, travelling back and forth between home and abroad becomes a mode of dwelling. Every movement between here and there bears with it a movement within a here and a movement within a there. In other words, the *return* is also a journey into the layer of '*future memory*' (Jelloun). The to-and-fro motion between the source and the activity of life is a motion within the source itself, which makes all activities of life possible. As regards Mother and Woman, she remains representatively singular (on His terms) – despite the very visible power of generalisation implied in the capitals M and W used here. For unless economical necessity forces her to leave the home on a daily basis, she is likely to be restrained in her mobility – a transcultural, class- and gender-specific practice that for centuries has not only made travelling quasi impossible for women, but has also compelled every 'travelling' female creature to become a stranger to her own family, society and gender.

It is said that when Florence Edenshaw, a contemporary Haida elder, was asked, 'What can I do for self-respect?' by a woman anthropologist who interviewed her and on whom Edenshaw's dignity made a strong impression, Edenshaw replied: 'Dress up and stay home.' Home seems to take on a peculiarly ambiguous resonance; so does the juxtaposition of 'dress' and 'stay'. One interpretation suggests that such a statement reflects the quiet dignity of members of non-state societies who rarely travel for the sake of some private quest, and deliberately risk themselves only when it is a question of the whole community's interest. Home then is as large as one makes it.[17] The profound respect for others starts with respect for oneself, as every individual carries the society within her. Read, however, against the background of what has been said earlier on Mother and Woman, Edenshaw's answer can also partake in the naturalised image of women as guardians of tradition, keepers of home and bearers of Language. The statement speaks of/to their lack of mobility in a male economy of movement. Women are trapped (as quoted) within the frontiers of their bodies and their species, and the general cliché by which they feel exiled here is the common consensus (in patriarchal societies) that streets and public places belong to men. Women are not supposed to circulate freely in these male domains, especially after dark (the time propitious to desire, 'the drive, the unnameable' and the unknown), for should anything happen to them that violates their physical well-being, they are immediately said to have 'asked for it' as they have singularly 'exposed' themselves by turning away from the Father's refuge. Yet Edenshaw's statement remains multi-levelled. It ultimately opens the door to a notion of self and home that invites the outside in, implies expansion through retreat, and is no more a movement inward than a movement outward, towards others. The stationariness conveyed in 'stay home' appears artificial – no more than a verbal limit – as 'stay' also means 'reach out'.

For a number of writers in exile, the true home is to be found not in houses but in writing. Such a perception may at first reading appear to contradict Kristeva's affirmation that 'writing is impossible without some kind of exile'. But home has proven to be both a place of confinement and an inexhaustible reservoir from which one can expand. And exile, despite its profound sadness, can be worked through as an experience of crossing boundaries and charting new ground in defiance of newly authorised or old canonical enclosures – 'a way of surviving in the face of the *dead father*'. Critical dissatisfaction has brought about a stretching of frontiers; home and exile in this context become as inseparable from each other as writing is from language. Writers who, in writing, open to research the space of language rather than reduce language to a mere instrument in the service of reason or feelings, are bound like the migrant to wander from country to country. They are said to be always lost to themselves, to belong to the foreign, and to be deprived of a true abode since, by their own passionate engagement with the tools that define their activities, they disturb the classical economy of language and representation, and can never be content with any stability of presence. Nothing remains unmoved; everything safe and sound is bound to sink somewhere in the process.

Their Country is My Country

Love, miss and grieve. This I can't simply deny. But I am a stranger to myself and a stranger now in a strange land. There is no arcane territory to return to. For I am no more an 'overseas' person in their land than in my own. Sometimes I see my country people as

complete strangers. But their country is my country. In the adopted
country, however, I can't go on being an exile or an immigrant either.
It's not a tenable place to be. I feel at once more in it and out of it.
Out of the named exiled, migrant, hyphenated, split self. The margin of
the centre. The Asian in America. The fragment of Woman. The Third
within the Second. Here too, Their country is My country. The source
continues to travel. The predicament of crossing boundaries cannot be
merely rejected or accepted. Again, if it is problematic to be a stranger,
it is even more so to stop being one. Colonised and marginalised
people are socialised to always see more than their own points of
view, and as Said phrases it, 'the essential privilege of exile is to have,
not just one set of eyes but half a dozen, each of them corresponding
to the places you have been ... There is always a kind of doubleness
to that experience, and the more places you have been the more
displacements you've gone through, as every exile does. As every
situation is a new one, you start out each day anew.'[18]

Despite the seemingly repetitive character of its theme and
variations, the tale of hyphenated reality continues its hybridising
process. It mutates in the repercussive course of its reproduction
as it multiplies and displaces itself from one context to another.
It is, in other words, always transient. But transience is precisely
what gives the tale its poignancy. Having grown despite heavy
odds in places where it was not meant to survive, this poetry of
marginalised people not only thrives on, but also persists in holding
its ground (no matter how fragile this ground proves to be) and
sometimes even succeeds in blooming wildly, remarkable in its
strange beauty and fabulous irregularity. Some familiar stories of
'mixed blessings' in America continue to be the following:

> So, here we are now, translated and invented skins, separated
> and severed like dandelions from the sacred and caught alive
> in words in the cities. We are aliens in our own traditions; the

white man has settled with his estranged words right in the middle of our sacred past. — Gerald Vizenor

I could tell you how hard it is to hide right in the midst of White people. It is an Art learned early because Life depends on dissimulation and harmlessness. To turn into a stone in the midst of snakes one pays a price. — Jack Forbes

Our people are internal exiles. To affirm that as a valid experience, when all other things are working against it, is a political act. That's the time when we stop being Mexican Americans and start being Chicanos. — Judy Baca

There is no doubt in my mind that the Asian American is on the doorstep of extinction. There's so much out-marriage now that all that is going to survive are the stereotypes. White culture has not acknowledged Asian American art. Either you're foreign in this country, or you're an honorary white. — Frank Chin

Sometimes / I want to forget it all / this curse called identity / I want to be far out / paint dreams in strange colors / write crazy poetry / only the chosen can understand / But it's not so simple / I still drink tea / with both hands. — Nancy Hom

If you're in coalition and you're comfortable, then it is not a broad enough coalition. — Bernice Johnson Reagon

The possibilities of meaning in 'I' are endless, vast, and varied because self-definition is a variable with at least five billion different forms ... [T]he I is one of the most particular, most unitary symbols, and yet it is one of the most general, most universal as well. — Cornelia Candelaria

I've avoided calling myself 'Indian' most of my life, even when
I have felt that identification most strongly, even when people
have called me an 'Indian.' Unlike my grandfather, I have
never seen that name as an insult, but there is another term
I like to use. I heard it first in Lakota and it refers to a person
of mixed blood, a metis. In English it becomes 'Translator's
Son.' It is not an insult, like half-breed. It means that you are
able to understand the language of both sides, to help them
understand each other. — Joseph Bruchac[19]

Translators' sons and daughters, or more redundantly, the
translators' translators. The source keeps on shifting. It is It that
travels. It is also I who carry a few fragments of it. Translations
mark the continuation of the original culture's life. As it has been
repeatedly proven, the hallmark of bad translation is to be found
in the inability to go beyond the mere imparting of information or
the transmittal of subject-matter. To strive for likeness to the
original – which is ultimately an impossible task – is to forget that
for something to live on, it has to be transformed. The original
is bound to undergo a change in its afterlife. Reflecting on the
translator's task, Benjamin remarked that: 'just as the tenor and
significance of the great works of literature undergo a complete
transformation over the centuries, the mother tongue of the
translator is transformed as well. While a poet's words endure in
his own language, even the greatest translation is destined to
become part of the growth of its own language and eventually to
be absorbed by its renewal.' Defined as a mode serving to express
the *relationship* between languages (rather than an equation
between two dead languages), translation is 'charged with the
special mission of watching over the maturing process of the
original language and the birth pangs of its own'.[20]

The Blue Frog

Identity is largely constituted through the process of othering. What can a return to the original be, indeed, when the original is always already somewhere other than where it is thought to be; when 'stay home' also means 'reach out', and native cultures themselves are constantly subject to intrinsic forms of translation? Here, Third is not merely derivative of First and Second. It is a space of its own. Such a space allows for the emergence of new subjectivities that resist letting themselves be settled in the movement across First and Second. Third is thus formed by the process of hybridisation which, rather than simply adding a here to a there, gives rise to an elsewhere-within-here/-there that appears both too recognisable and impossible to contain. Vietnamese francophone poet and novelist Pham Van Ky, for example, raises the problematics of translated hyphenated realities specifically in the following terms:

> Mother. A word released, a word with precise contours, which crushes me but does not cover me up entirely, but does not articulate my Parisian existence; already a decision hardens within me ... this abyss of secrets, reticences, obscurities, hollow dreams and foul haze between Mother and me: nothing clear, a series of disagreements, of bitter trails where grass never grows, a chain of vague pains jumping at my wrist and around my chest, seeking to restrain my breathing and the circulation of my blood ... In the Bois de Vincennes, I reread the cablegram: Mother seemed near me. I tried to draw her closer to me: she became distant again. Because I had forgotten about her, did I feel less tied to her by life? Why conceal her from myself? She had carried me in her hemorrhage; I did not pull out a single hair, which was not a bit, hers.[21]

Another instance of working with between-world reality is that of Elaine K. Chang, who, in an attempt to situate herself (via an essay significantly entitled: 'A Not-So-New Spelling of My Name: Notes Toward (and Against) a Politics of Equivocation'), has this unique story of travelling metaphor to offer:

> Within the North American 'Asian community', I am sometimes called a banana; it is said that I may have a yellow skin, but I am white on the inside. I am considered ashamed of my yellowness, insofar as I apparently aspire to master the language, culture and ideology of white people. *Banyukja* is ... a Korean translation of the Spanish *vendida* – the Korean who has forgotten, or never known, her heritage, her language ... I cannot properly answer to these names, especially to and in a language I have lost. I cannot tell those for whom I am a banana, or worse a *banyukja*, that my exile from them is not entirely self-imposed, that I am not ashamed and have not forgotten. Nor can I respond in so many English or broken Korean words that the ignorance they ascribe to men, the silence they expect from me, themselves cooperate to estrange me: that what I do understand of what they say serves to alienate me ... If I could rename myself ... I think I would have to select a figure not female, not divine, not even human: the blue frog. My mother's story about the blue frog was my favorite childhood story. The blue frog never does anything his mother tells him to do; in fact he does precisely the opposite. I pestered my mother to tell the story over and over; each time she told it, the frog-mother's requests and the blue frog's responses seemed to become more outrageous. The ending, however, remained soberly the same. Loving and knowing her son, and knowing she is about to die, the frog-mother makes her last request: that her son bury her body in the river – of

course thinking her son, due to his contrary nature, will bury her in the ground. When his mother dies, however, the blue frog is so remorseful for his life-long disobedience that he chooses to observe her final wishes. So every time it rains, the blue frog cries, thinking that his mother's body is washing away in the river.

It wasn't until I was considerably older, and she had not told the story for years, that I asked my mother if she remembered the little blue frog. Confused at first, she remembered after I'd recapitulated the basic plot structure. Blushing, my mother informed me that the frog was not, in fact, blue; she had not yet mastered colors in English when she first told me the story. Old as I was, I was crushed by this information: it was all along just some ordinary green frog. What had compelled me about this particular frog – this frog whose story quite accurately ... resembles the story of my relationship with my mother – was his blueness ... I would invoke the blue frog as my inspiration because of this coding and recoding of the color of his skin; the ambiguity of his color registers the sorts of small but significant ironies that distinguish my experience as a westernized child of immigrant parents. My mother shared with me a Korean folktale that acquired something new in its translation into English ... The blue frog is a (by-)product of cultural and linguistic cross-fertilization – a small and mundane one, to be sure, but one that I would take as my emblem – Do blue frogs have a place in academic discourse?[22]

Tale-telling is what it takes to expose motherhood in all its ambivalence. The boundaries of identity and difference are continually repositioned in relation to varying points of reference. The meanings of here and there, home and abroad, third and first, margin and centre keep on being displaced according to how one positions oneself.

Where is 'home'? Mother continues to exert her power from afar. Even in her absence she is present within the teller, his blood, his source of life. From one generation to another, mothers are both condemned and called upon to perfect their role as the killjoy keepers of home and of tradition. In Kristeva's fable of dissidence, Mother (with capital M) may be said to partake in the 'mire of common sense' (common to whom?) and to represent Meaning as established by the 'dead father'. Therefore, it is by resisting Her powers of generalisation that a woman becomes a stranger to her own language, sex and identity. In Jelloun's tale of time, Mother is the benevolent travelling source that, in fact, does not travel on her own. She is, rather, the transmitter of 'a body full of sentences, proverbs and noises' and the originator of the 'warm fabric of [his] memory' that 'shelters and nourishes [him]'. Like language, mother (with small m) retains her secrets and it is through her son that she travels and continues to live on – albeit in fragments.

For Pham Van Ky, Mother is what he fiercely rejects without feeling any less tied to her by life. In a conventional gender division, she – the guardian of tradition – represents his Oriental, Vietnamese, Confucian past and the Far East over there; while he – the promoter of modernity – can go on representing change and progress, and the Far West over here. But as he admits to himself, mother can neither be discarded nor easily appropriated: 'I did not pull out a single hair which was not a bit hers.' In fact, the travelling seed has never had an original location that could simply be returned to. For Elaine Chang, Mother is the imperfect transmitter of a folktale whose voyage in time, across language and generation, has allowed it to acquire something new in its translation. The coding and recoding of the skin colour of the frog speak to the sadness (/blueness) of both the daughter's and the frog's inappropriate experience of translation. In both cases, mistranslation results from a two-way imperfection in the triangular relationship of mother, child and language. The source is never single, and the home-and-abroad or land-and-water trajectory is a mutual voyage into self and other. Travelling in what appear to be opposite directions, the two parties only meet when 'meet' also comes to mean 'lose' – that is, when mother or the story can no longer be returned to as redemptive site. Understanding and consciousness emerge in one case, when the frog realises its mistake in carrying out a literal translation of his mother's request after she has passed away; and in the other case, when the daughter's natural identification with the blue frog comes to an end to make way for a 'politics of equivocation' in the articulation of hyphenated identity. The ability to assume anew the responsibility of translation thereby opens up to an elsewhere, at once not-yet- and too-well-named within the process of cultural and linguistic cross-fertilisation.

I, the Mis-seer

Every voyage is the unfolding of a poetic. The departure, the crossover, the fall, the wandering, the discovery, the return, the transformation. If travelling perpetuates a discontinuous state of being, it also satisfies, despite the existential difficulties it often entails, one's insatiable need for detours and displacements in postmodern culture. The complex experience of self and other (the all-other within me and without me) is bound to forms that belong but are subject neither to 'home', nor to 'abroad'; and it is through them and through the cultural configurations they gather that the universe over there and over here can be named, accounted for, and become narrative. Travellers' tales do not only bring the over-there home, and the over-here abroad. They do not only bring the far away within reach, but also contribute, as discussed, to challenging the home and abroad/dwelling and travelling dichotomy within specific actualities. At best, they speak to the problem of the impossibility of packaging a culture, or of defining an authentic cultural identity.

For cultures whose expansion and dominance were intimately dependent upon the colonial enterprise, travelling, as part of a system of foreign investment by metropolitan powers, has largely been a form of culture-collecting aimed at world hegemony. In their critical relation to such a journeying practice, a number of European writers[23] have thus come to see in travelling a socio-historical process of dispossession that leads the contemporary traveller to a real identity crisis. Through this 'nightmare of degradation', the Traveller seems to have become so banal, outdated and disintegrated in certain images he projects that it is not unusual to ask whether he is still ... a possibility. One among some fifty million globetrotters, the Traveller maintains his difference mostly by despising others like him. I sneeze at organised tours, for the things I see in the Wild or in the remote parts of the world, are those You can't see when You abide by pre-paid, ready-made routes. Furthermore, You don't see all that I know how to see, even if You go to the same places. In the arguments used here to preserve one's difference, there is an eager attempt to define one's activities by negating them. The role of the traveller as privileged seer and knowledgeable observer has thus become quasi impossible, for it is said that the real period of Travelling always seems to be already past, and the other travellers are always bound to be 'tourists'.[24]

The search for 'micro-deserts', the need to ignore or the desire to go beyond the beaten tracks of pre-packaged tours is always reactivated. Travelling here inscribes itself as a deviance within a circularly saturated space. Adventure can only survive in the small empty spaces of intervals and interstices. As soon as something is told, there is nothing more to discover and to tell, so it is believed. All that remains for the real Traveller is 'the privilege of a certain look, in the margin of the Standard Point of View as signalled in the tourist Guides'. Constantly evoked, therefore, are the blindness and myopia of the Tourist, whose voracity in consuming cultures as commodities has made hardship and adventure in travelling a necessary part of pre-planned excitement rather than a mere hindrance. Cultural tourism is thus said to challenge the dichotomy that separates the expert Ethnologist from the non-expert Tourist. 'The traditional Traveller's tragedy is that he is an imitable and imitated explorer.' Therefore, in order not to be confused with the Tourist, the Traveller has to become clandestine. He has to *imitate* the Other, to hide and disguise himself in an attempt to inscribe himself in a counter-exoticism that will allow him to be a non-Tourist – that is, someone who no longer resembles his falsified other, hence a stranger to his own kind.[25]

Ironically enough, it is by turning himself into another falsified other (in imitating the Other) that the Traveller succeeds in marking himself off from his falsified other (the Tourist). He who is easily imitable and imitated now takes on the role of the imitator to survive. The process of othering in the (de)construction of identity continues its complex course. Rather than contributing to a radical questioning of the privileged seer, however, the Traveller's 'identity crisis' often leads to a mere change of appearance – a temporary disguise whose narrative remains, at best, a Confession. As discussed earlier, striving for likeness to the original without being powerfully affected by the foreigner (the Other) is the hallmark of bad translation. The Traveller as imitator may perform the task of a faithful reproducer of meaning, but to become a (good) translator, he would have 'to expand and deepen his language by means of the foreign language'.[26] To travel can consist in operating a profoundly unsettling inversion of one's identity: I become me via an other. Depending on who is looking, the exotic is the other, or it is I. For the one who is off- and outside culture, is not the one over there whose familiar culture I am still a part of, or whose unfamiliar culture I come to learn from. I am the one making a detour with myself, having left upon my departure from over here not only a place but also one of my selves. The itinerary displaces the foundation; the background of my identity, and what it incessantly unfolds is the very encounter of self with the other – other than myself and, my other self.

In travelling, one is a being-for-other, but also a being-*with*-other. The seer is seen while s/he sees. To see and to be seen constitute the double approach of identity: the presence to oneself is at once impossible and immediate. 'I can't produce by myself the stranger's strangeness: it is born from [at least] two looks.'[27] Travelling allows one to see things differently from what they are, differently from how one has seen them, and differently from what one is. These three supplementary identities gained via alterity are in fact still (undeveloped or unrealised) gestures of the 'self' – the energy system that defines (albeit in a shifting and contingent mode) what and who each seer is. The voyage out of the (known) self and back into the (unknown) self sometimes takes the wanderer far away to a motley place where everything safe and sound seems to waver, while the essence of language is placed in doubt and profoundly destabilised. Travelling can thus turn out to be a process whereby the self loses its fixed boundaries – a disturbing yet potentially empowering practice of difference.

'The word is more important than syntax ... It is the blanks that impose themselves ... I am telling you how it happens, it is the blanks that appear, perhaps under the stroke of a violent rejection of syntax ... [T]he place where it writes itself, where one writes ... is a place where breathing is rarefied, there is a diminution of sensorial acuity ...'

'Would a man, in his sexuality, show the blank just like that? Because it's also sexual, this blank, this emptiness.'

'No, I don't think so; he would intervene. I myself do not intervene.'[28]

It seems clear, for writers like Marguerite Duras, who lets herself return to 'a wild country' when she writes, that one can only gain insight by letting oneself go blind as one gropes one's way through the oversaid and the all-too-clear of one's language. 'Men are regressing everywhere, in all areas', she remarked. 'The theoretical sphere is losing influence ... it should lose itself in a reawakening of the senses, blind itself, and be still.' For scarcely has an important event been experienced before men, always eager to act as theoretical policemen, 'begin to speak out, to formulate theoretical epilogues, and to break the silence ... [H]ere silence is precisely the sum of the voices of everyone, the equivalent of the sum of our collective breathing ... And this collective silence was necessary because it would have been through this silence that a new mode of being would have been fostered.' Duras called such arresting of the flow of silence 'a crime and a masculine one', for if it has in innumerable cases stifled the voices of the marginalised others, it has in her own case certainly made her 'nauseous at the thought of any activism after 1968'.[29]

If the space of language is to resonate anew, if I am to speak differently, He must learn to be silent – He, the Traveller who is in me and in woman. For s/he who thinks s/he sees best because s/he *knows* how to see is also this conscientious 'mis-seer to whom the tree hides the forest'.[30] Without perspectives, deaf and myopic to everything that is not microscopic, the non-tourist-real-traveller operates, often *unknowingly*, in a realm of diminished sensorial acuity. On the one hand, s/he develops a highly refined ear and eye for close readings, but remains oblivious to the landscape and the 'built environment' which make the traveller-seer's activities possible and communicable. On the other hand, deliberate mis-seeing is necessitated to bring about a different form of seeing. When the look is 'a three-way imperfection' developed between the subject observed, the subject observing, and the tools for observation, the encounter is likely to resonate in strangely familiar and unpredictable ways. The translator transforms while being transformed. Imperfection thus leads to new realms of exploration, and travelling as a practice of bold omission and minute depiction allows one to (become) shamelessly hybridise(d) as one shuttles back and forth between critical blindness and critical insight. I-the-Seer is bound to mis-see so as to unlearn the privilege of seeing, and while I travel, what I see in every ordinary green frog is, undeniably, my blueness in the blue frog. In the zest of telling, I thus find myself translating myself by quoting all others. The travelling tales.

—

1 Tahar Ben Jelloun, 'Les Pierres du temps', *Traverses*, 40: *Théâtres de la mémoire* (April 1987), p. 158. Unless indicated otherwise, all translations from the French are the author's.
2 Gary Snyder, *The Practice of the Wild* (San Francisco: Northpoint Press, 1990), p. 7.
3 Jelloun, 'Les Pierres du temps', p. 159.
4 Tahar Ben Jelloun, *Moha le fou, Moha le sage* (Paris: Seuil, 1978), p. 10.
5 Maurice Blanchot, *Vicious Circles*, trans. P. Auster (Barrytown, NY: Station Hill Press, 1985), p. 19.
6 Edward Said, 'Reflections on Exile', in *Out There: Marginalization and Contemporary Culture*, ed. Russell Ferguson et al. (New York: The New Museum of Contemporary Art and MIT Press, 1990), pp. 357–58.
7 Quoted in Bruce Grant et al., *The Boat People: An 'Age' Investigation* (New York: Penguin, 1979), p. 182.
8 Quoted ibid., p. 173.
9 Ibid., p. 195.
10 Terms used by a Halifax woman with regards to Canada and the flux of Southeast Asian refugees in the late 1970s, reported ibid., p. 174.
11 Blanchot, *Vicious Circles*, p. 66.
12 Julia Kristeva, 'A New Type of Intellectual: The Dissident', in *The Kristeva Reader*, ed. Toril Moi (New York: Columbia University Press, 1986), pp. 298, 296, original italics.
13 Ibid., p. 286.
14 Quoted in Hannah Arendt's introduction in Walter Benjamin, *Illuminations*, trans. Harry Zohn (New York: Schocken Books, 1969), p. 20.
15 Said, 'Reflections on Exile', p. 357.
16 Ibid., pp. 364–65, original italics.

17 Snyder, *Practice of the Wild*, pp. 23–24.
18 Edward Said, 'The Voice of a Palestinian in Exile', *Third Text*, 3–4 (Spring/Summer 1988), p. 48.
19 All quoted in Lucy R. Lippard, *Mixed Blessings: New Art in a Multicultural America* (New York: Pantheon, 1990), pp. 23, 30, 170, 47, 41, 151.
20 Benjamin, *Illuminations*, p. 73.
21 Pham Van Ky, *Des femmes assises çà et là* (Paris: Gallimard, 1964), pp. 8, 18. The quoted passage was translated in Jack A. Yeager, *The Vietnamese Novel in French: A Literary Response to Colonialism* (Hanover, NH: University Press of New England, 1986), pp. 151–52.
22 Elaine K. Chang, 'A Not-So-New Spelling of My Name: Notes Toward (and Against) a Politics of Equivocation', in *Displacement: Cultural Identities in Question*, ed. Angelika Bammer (Bloomington, IN: Indiana University Press, 1994), pp. 251–66.
23 See, for example, the articles published in *Traverses*, 41–42: *Voyages* (September 1987), more particularly those written by J.-C. Guillebaud, J.-D. Urbain, P. Curvel, P. Virilio, V. Vadsaria, P. Sansot, C. Wulf, F. Affergan and C. Reichler.
24 See Jonathan Culler, 'Semiotics of Tourism', *American Journal of Semiotics*, 1–2 (1981), p. 130.
25 Jean-Didier Urbain, 'Le Voyageur detrousse', *Traverses*, 41–42: *Voyages* (September 1987), pp. 43, 48.
26 Benjamin, *Illuminations*, p. 81.
27 Christoph Wulf, 'La Voie lactée', *Traverses*, 41–42: *Voyages* (September 1987), p. 128.
28 Marguerite Duras interviewed by Xavière Gauthier in *Les Parleuses* (Paris: Éditions de Minuit, 1974), pp. 11–12.
29 Marguerite Duras in Elaine Marks and Isabelle de Courtivron, eds, *New French Feminisms: An Anthology* (Amherst, MA: University of Massachusetts Press, 1980), pp. 111–12.
30 Jean-Claude Guillebaud, 'Une ruse de la littérature', *Traverses*, 41–42: *Voyages* (September 1987), p. 16.

WOMAN WITH A MOVIE CAMERA

XIAOLU GUO

When Leni Riefenstahl died, she was 101 years old. It was a September morning in 2003. I was 29 years old, a documentary filmmaker newly arrived from China, hungry for cinema and for Western life. That very morning, I was walking along Marylebone Road in London, trying to get some breakfast before taking my train to the film school in Beaconsfield.

Only recently arrived in England, I knew nothing about London or the National Film and Television School in this country. All I knew was that the school was not far from Pinewood Studios, where David Lean had made his *Oliver Twist* in the 1940s. That morning, as I sat down in a café called Billy's, gulping down my first coffee and waiting for baked beans on toast, I heard the radio news: 'One of the world's most famous woman filmmakers and actresses, Leni Riefenstahl, has died at her home in Bavaria. She had recently celebrated her 101st birthday.'

I was surprised by the news, and almost shocked to learn her age. We had studied Riefenstahl's cinema back in film school in China, but I was not aware that she had been alive all these years. Like an iconic black-and-white photo, she had been stuck in the past, in the Nazi period. During my studies, her place in film history was vague but seemed generally positive, and her situation was not as politicised as it is in the West. As an artist, she was notorious for her so called 'glorious' years in the Third Reich, with Hitler at the centre of her images. *Olympia* (1938) was one of the films we had to analyse – as much as we did Orson Welles's *Citizen Kane* (1941). But I had never thought about her life after the war. How had she managed to survive the sweeping forces of German history? My breakfast arrived as the radio went on, explaining that although Riefenstahl was put on trial four times as a Nazi propagandist, she was never convicted as she claimed she hadn't known anything about the Holocaust. 'She remained free and is still recognised as a genius of cinema. Coming next, the weather forecast ...'

I swallowed my baked beans, forgetting to chew. This news pulled the pin off the hand grenade of my mind. As a Chinese person who had never lived in the West, I had thought very little about this controversial artist: a dancer and an actress originally, then a marvellous filmmaker and a photographer. I remember at the Beijing Film Academy in the 1990s, along with her *Olympia*, we also studied *Triumph of the Will* (1935), almost scene by scene. We were told to pay attention to the contrast between close-ups and wide shots, as well as the montage. But our professors barely discussed its political background. Yes, Hitler was a problem. But propaganda was not necessarily a problem. Because in China and elsewhere in East Asia, there are thousands of films like *Triumph of the Will*, used to show the power of politics and ideologies. *Olympia* is another propaganda film – about absolute physical beauty and strength. The language of propaganda in the visual arts was the norm in our recent history. It was almost the 'automatic' and 'naturalistic' artistic language of contemporary Chinese cinema.

In Marylebone train station, along with dozens of commuting office workers, I jumped on my train, heading towards Beaconsfield. The satellite towns of London appeared one after another in their almost uniform rusty-brown existence: Harrow on the Hill, South Ruislip, West Ruislip, Denham, Gerrards Cross ... Then suddenly, a train of enchanted black-and-white images formed themselves in front of those towns. Those images were from one of the most beautiful films I had ever seen: Riefenstahl's *The Blue Light* (1932). The young, fresh, fairy-like Junta, played by Riefenstahl, sits by a waterfall in a dark forest, watching the bright moon above her while the hostile world lies dreamless beneath. I thought of how those images combined to build my idea of the northern European landscape and the picture of blonde people in my imagination. The heroine in the film lives away from the mean and nasty villagers, spending her days on the cliffs and in the valleys.

The wild, mysterious life of this Western girl was, in a sense, the fantasy of my childhood. How I had wanted to escape my village in south China, and how I wished to hide in the mountains and live freely by myself. Under the moonlight, Riefenstahl's illuminated eyes were so pure and angelic, suggesting that she would be crushed by the hostile world of the village. Riefenstahl was 29-and-a-half while she directed and performed in the film. Exactly the age I was now, on that train to Beaconsfield. When and where would I find my own blue light? It must be somewhere – if not in a northern forest, then out there in this world, most probably outside my own country.

But perhaps I misread the message in *The Blue Light*. It is actually a film about a fallen angel, a female antichrist. I read somewhere that it was Hitler who first fell in love with Riefenstahl – not the other way around. Hitler watched *The Blue Light* and was mesmerised by the beauty of the film as well as its heroine. It was his favourite German film then. Deeply affected by the spirituality of the landscape and the depiction of the wild girl, he followed Riefenstahl's career. He watched other films acted and directed by her and was totally enchanted by her power. Finally he asked her to make films for him. But in other versions of the history, it is the other way around: Riefenstahl was drawn to Hitler first. It is in fact recorded that way in her own memoir, published in Germany in 1987. After attending a Nazi rally in Berlin in 1932 and hearing Hitler give a speech, she wrote him a passionate letter asking about the possibility of a meeting. And that was the beginning of her career as perhaps the most infamous propaganda artist of all time.

As the cities and little towns gradually disappeared from sight, the English countryside was unfolding in front of me. Goats and sheep, farmhouses and wheat fields appeared in the distance. My memory travelled further back. I recalled one of the first Western films I ever saw in my Chinese province. It was the 1980s and we lived next to the People's Auditorium of our town. One day, the cinema was showing a black-and-white foreign film dubbed into Chinese. It was *Limelight* (1952) by Charlie Chaplin, with the Chinese title 舞台生涯, meaning 'Life on the Stage'. I was about ten and didn't know who Charlie Chaplin was. Throughout the film, I was confused by this clown character with a moustache. Sometimes he looked very noble to me, at other times he appeared lost and miserable, like a beggar. I found the young ballerina character intriguing. For the first half of the film, she only sits on her bed reminiscing about her past while the clown attends to her; then, with his help, she gets out of her bed. She is saved by him and becomes a great dancer again. But how unfair the world seems to be, I thought. Why does the old clown have to die in the end, yet the girl has everything she wanted, including her young lover! My sympathy went to the Chaplin character, and the film left a sad impression on me. The idea that 'beauty is more important than kindness' somehow stayed with me. Having vaguely learned that the story was set in London – somewhere far away in a foreign land – I was told by my father that the clown actor was also the director of the film, and that he was banned from entering the United States because he was a 'communist sympathiser'. 'What's wrong being a communist sympathiser?' I asked my father. As far as I knew, every decent person in my hometown was a communist: my father, my uncles, their colleagues and friends; only peasants and non-educated people were not communists then. And as soon as I grew up, I thought, I would join the party and become a communist too. The only thing my father explained to me was: 'The Americans are imperialists. Communists are their enemies.'

Of course, that answer led to even deeper confusion. In my little head, communists were workers and proletarians who work very hard and dress poorly. But in that film, the clown and the ballerina all wear beautiful outfits and live in very fancy places. They don't seem to need to labour in fields or work in factories. Their lifestyle seemed to be un-communist, its opposite in fact. So what made them so communist? Or was Western communism very different from Chinese communism? But my father did not explain further.

Along with *Limelight*, one of the Western films I watched at that time was a film about the Yugoslav leader Tito and his heroic revolutionary acts. Like others in China, I adored Tito too. I also watched a number of films about Chinese Red Army soldiers fighting the Nationalist army. As far as I can remember, there was no film I had seen that didn't have a communist revolutionary story. But *Limelight* seemed to be the first film I'd ever seen without gun smoke and heroes dying in explosions while shouting out a final grand slogan. Tito did not stay very long in my heart, but the Chaplin film made me curious about life as an artist, a life away from smoke and bombs, a life full of music, dance and imagination, just like the clown and the ballerina in the film.

The train stopped at Beaconsfield station, where I would get off. I exited from the carriage. Today I would have a class on camera work, and another class on editing. I would be doing workshops, exercising wide angles, practising focus-pulling and movements during shooting. What kind of filmmaker would I become? Would I be a woman with a movie camera, out there in the streets, observing the world through my viewfinder? And what kind of aesthetic and political position would I adopt? With all these questions in my head, I walked past rows of English country houses, entering the gates of the film school.

After my days in Beaconsfield, I became a filmmaker. I wrote and directed all my films. Some were filmed in the West, but most were shot in China and then edited in Europe with Western post-production teams. Often I thought of Leni Riefenstahl, especially during the editing process. I thought about her aesthetics and her way of conducting the film crew. But mostly, I thought of her being a state artist. I thought of my own stateless status as a filmmaker. One can be an exiled writer for the rest of one's life, but not an exiled filmmaker, at least not for very long. Because to make a reasonably decent film, especially a fiction feature, one needs financial support – whether from state or independent sources. Also, one needs an audience with a shared cultural background and linguistic familiarity. Since I had left China, and since my books were not especially friendly to my native country, I could not get any support from my country. Nor could I receive any Western funding without years of waiting and begging. After struggling for some years, I made fewer and fewer films, and I turned to novel writing. If I ever got the chance to make a film, it was always a humble-looking guerrilla movie, involving me holding a home video camera, accompanied by my credit card. Exquisite aesthetic control in filmmaking seems to me a long-gone, privileged, bourgeois activity, not to mention hiring actors or sets, or possessing an audience that comes from my cultural background. On the other hand, I enjoyed the freedom I had gained through the topics and ways of making my films, in exchange for the punishment of no production value, no distribution at all.

 I think of my dead father, who was a state painter all his life in China. He was given a large painting studio and was paid by the state, including housing and healthcare. He did not need to worry about living, as long as he could convince himself to forget about the bitter years he spent in a labour camp. He did not always need to paint a revolutionary subject, but only keep quiet about his political opinions. I cannot know entirely how my father managed to live and to paint all those years. The cancer had always been threatening his life, and he spent more than a third of it coping with the illness. I had never wanted his kind of life. I thought it was a golden cage. But decades later, after I had struggled to make my own films in the West and after I knew I was never going to return to China, I was desperate for some support. Any support, whether state or private. I thought of the possibility of being a state artist. I realised that those filmmakers I had admired, such as Sergei Eisenstein and

Dziga Vertov, were state artists. One can even argue that Jean-Luc Godard or Agnès Varda were practically state artists too, given their funding came mostly from public funds – though state-supported artists are not necessarily state artists. Obviously Godard and Varda worked in a Western democratic and counter-hegemonic style, something neither Eisenstein or Vertov could possibly achieve.

My ideal work environment would be the one resembling Godard and Varda's. But this was a dream beyond any Chinese artist's imagination. Where could I belong in the West? I could not get any help, professionally or privately. But if there were a historical twist, would a filmmaker like me for the sake of her career do something like Riefenstahl did? To evaluate her life as an artist, one has to think of an artist in and out of state favour. She was a state artist until the end of Hitler's rule, and she then fell into obscurity as a non-state artist – in fact, a potential state enemy for the rest of her life. It was quite a phenomenon that during her multiple trials she defended herself in a more or less convincing way. She insisted that she had not been aware of the nature of the concentration camps. Shortly before she died, Riefenstahl said in a BBC interview: 'I was one of millions who thought Hitler had all the answers. We saw only the good things; we didn't know bad things were to come.' There might be some truth in her claim, though she could not have been totally innocent. I also thought that her later films, especially the underwater ones, were uninteresting, in fact rather banal. The films were devoid of any human reality or trace of political thinking.

Her disappearance from the film industry always brought to mind that mysterious term that the Allies used about her in the denazification period: in German a *Mitläufer*, a 'fellow traveller'. It's an almost poetic way to describe someone who sympathised with the Nazis during the war in this way. A glorious artist was only a 'fellow traveller' in the judgement of history. It's troubling that the incredible power relation between artist and state, as well as the destructiveness it so easily engenders, should be reduced to this word. A *Mitläufer*. It reminds us that it is not good enough to be a woman with a movie camera. What's important is for a woman to have a thoroughly disabused historical vision which will allow her camera to point in the right direction.

A LONG-FORGOTTEN IMAGE

JULIETTE JOFFÉ

We met the day I came back to Paris.

Many years had passed since I left. I didn't know where to start and spent a very long time staring at the different routes on the Métro map. At random, I picked the green line and when the Eiffel Tower appeared through the window, I mechanically got off the train as if attracted by a magnet.

I blindly followed a guide leading a tourist crowd, speaking words I couldn't understand into a voice amplifier. There was something comforting about being part of a group of strangers. I became one of them and imitated everyone else: I took pictures.

At noon we were in Montmartre watching the city from above. So many fingers pointed towards the city: 'Here Notre-Dame', 'There the Tour Montparnasse'. Kids were directing giant binoculars towards the sky.

Did I used to do that?

Looking at the city, I was reminded of the reason I was here. The Parc Montsouris. I rushed towards a giant binocular that had just been abandoned by chubby fingers.

Where was it again? Which green patch in this endless landscape?

A stranger said I should get off at Cité Universitaire on RER B. I stared again at the train map; it seemed like the right place.

Thirty minutes later I had reached my destination and picked a bench in front of the carousel. Only one kid was riding it, on a giant cat's back. Her mother kept paying for her to go on new rides and the child turned around endlessly, as if performing her daily routine.

I took my camera out to take a picture of what I thought might be the carousel of my childhood. I waited for the giant cat and its rider to enter the frame. Just as I pressed the camera button, you stood in front of my lens and took the picture I wanted.

The first thing I said to you was: 'You took my picture.'

You turned around towards me and pressed your camera's button. 'Now I did.'

You sat on the bench next to me and told me you were Yuya, a translator from Japan. I remember you asked: 'Why did you want to take this picture?'

This is how we got to know each other. Talking about the picture we both wanted.

'I grew up here, I am from here,' I said.

It wasn't a good enough answer. So you asked more questions. But before doing so, you said you had translated *Enfance* (*Childhood*) by Nathalie Sarraute from French to Japanese, and explained: 'Sarraute also grew up here; in the book she writes about fragments of her childhood, some of which take place in this park.'

'Fragments' of my childhood; was that what I had come here to look for? you asked.

My response, to avoid answering you: 'Are you looking for the child that Sarraute once was?'

We both looked at each other's cameras suspiciously, before starting a very long discussion that was to last hours, months. From this first conversation I only remember bits, sentences, impressions, images.

At some point I answered your first question, or maybe I just gave you a clue to decode: 'Something happened in this park which left a big black hole in my memory. I am here to uncover what this event was.'

Much later in the conversation, and with no relation at all to my sentence cited above, you said, while showing me one of your pictures of the park: 'I believe it was here that Vera, Sarraute's stepmother, told her when she was only seven years old, "Tiebia podobroslili" – *You have been abandoned*. Sarraute used to go to the Parc Montsouris with Vera, her father and her newborn sibling. For many years, she lived away from her mother, who had remained in Russia. For her, this place was tainted with melancholia, as described in *Enfance*.'

How many solitary walks through the park have you had before reaching this conclusion? I thought.

Later or before these lines:

Me: 'We both seem to be looking for childhoods.'

You: 'With the help of a camera. Why do we need pictures?'

Me: 'To help us see better, or remember better, or find clues?'

You: 'Maybe we can help each other.'

You again: 'Sarraute's concept of "tropism" suggests that below our consciousness we all have a similar base from which our personalities emerge. However different our quests are, we are all formed from the same substance.'

At some point in this conversation, you invited me to the House of Japan, a place for Japanese students in the Cité Universitaire, a park made only of residences from every country, and conceived in 1925 for foreigners studying in Paris. It was the perfect place for you to stay; it seemed like it belonged in the past and it was just in front of the Parc Montsouris.

Your walls were covered with pictures of the park; in most of them were women from all ages. I was in one of them. Sarraute was in none. Or was she a combination of all of them? In another one, a parade of musicians.

Me: 'I also took a picture of this parade. The only thing I remember from the day *it* happened is the sound of a parade.'

You: 'Who knows, I might stumble without searching upon one of your memories.'

Yes, I thought, they are everywhere here. I grew up here, I forgot everything here. I lived and fell into a black hole. If you walk the park long enough, you might see or feel it.

I have already asked so many people sitting on these benches or lying on the grass: 'Do you remember? Were you here on the day of the parade?'

Some of these strangers' faces might be those of people I used to play with as a child. Maybe they recognised me for a glimpse of a second before I returned to being an entirely unknown face to them.

A week later I flew back to Australia. The first letter you sent me started with:

I didn't tell you in Paris, but when we met, it felt like I had seen you before. Strangers' faces sometimes seem familiar. Yet, most of the time we can never recollect where we have encountered them before. Since you left it has only been snowing. I am often the only person in the park, with my camera as sole companion. It is strange how a place can absorb us until we get totally lost in it, in the unfolding of its many routes.

My last letter to you ended with:

Before you go back to Japan, I will visit you in Paris. How else can I thank you for helping me remember a long-forgotten image, buried by my own hands. Sometimes it is much easier to gaze at what is closest to us and most painful through a stranger's eyes. Emmanuelle Riva in *Hiroshima mon amour* confides in her recently met Japanese lover about her trauma of humiliation during World War Two.

She hardly knows him.

Yet at this instant, only he can help her by being the recipient of her story.

Both are unnamed, lovers, strangers, witnesses.

They have lived the same war on opposite sides of the globe. They haven't seen what the other has seen.

He keeps telling her: 'You have seen nothing in Hiroshima.'
Yet as he listens and immerses himself into her words, I like to believe they have shared these remote experiences.

Thank you for your help,

J

THE STRANGERS WITHIN US

DAVID MACDOUGALL

We are made up of fragments of others, in body and spirit. We inherit the genetic characteristics of our ancestors. We learn to speak a language from our parents and childhood friends. In food and drink, we absorb the properties of the material things around us. If, as they say, we are what we eat, it is not surprising that we also become what we see, and form ourselves in our connections with others.

This principle has been supported by neuroscientists, who have found that seeing the actions or expressed emotions of another person activates some of the same responses in ourselves, if only subliminally.[1] It suggests that human societies are not made up of dispersed individuals but are in some ways more like groups of social animals such as bees, ants and corals. Those of us who as artists, actors, writers or filmmakers observe others closely sometimes have the disconcerting sense of being suffused by their presence. It is as if for a time we put our own consciousness aside and become intermixed with theirs. Later we may discover ourselves using a gesture or turn of phrase that is not our own. This can haunt us for days until we identify where and when we first encountered it.

An impression of being both outside and inside another human being is a common experience for filmmakers, especially those making biographical or portrait films.[2] Over weeks and even months the filmmaker is 'exposed' to the person and registers their qualities like the film in a camera. Filmmakers learn to move with the subject and anticipate their actions and responses. They become acutely aware of the subject's mannerisms, how they move, their facial expressions, specific details of their appearance, the timbre of their voice and their characteristic ways of speaking. It is not surprising that under these circumstances the subject's living presence enters increasingly into their imagination. A filmmaker may even feel a partial loss of his or her own personal identity. How these displacements of being are possible can perhaps be grasped from the way that, as onlookers at a tennis match or other sports event, we move unconsciously with the body movements of the players and share emotionally in their successes and disappointments.

Such a sympathetic relationship is not always the case, however. In the making of portrait films the relations between filmmakers and their subjects can vary greatly, from the mutual antagonism between Nick Broomfield and Eugène Terre'Blanche in *The Leader, His Driver and the Driver's Wife* (1991), to D. A. Pennebaker's somewhat offhand curiosity about Bob Dylan in *Don't Look Back* (1967), to the intensity of Johan van der Keuken's depiction of the girl in his film *Beppie* (1965). The length of exposure may be crucial. Some portrait films take years to complete, while others are made in a few days. In films about celebrities and public figures there may be no contact at all between filmmaker and subject, whereas many other films involve close personal relationships. Some film subjects contribute little to the project; others collaborate extensively in it. In a few further cases a close but tacit understanding develops between subject and filmmaker, a form of collaboration that I have termed 'symbiosis'.

For many makers of portrait films there is a strong underlying desire for a film somehow to embody its subject, by capturing not only the person's physical appearance but also a sense of their living presence. This comes partly from having observed the subject closely over a period of time and partly from having sensed the potential for such immediacy in other films. It is not uncommon when watching a film to feel someone vividly present even when they are now long gone. In film after film, actors like Humphrey Bogart, Simone Signoret, Ingrid Bergman and Jean Gabin continue to convey their distinctive personalities to us, projected across the gulf of time, geography and an imperfect technology. In documentary films as well, we may feel we have had an almost physical brush with a living person, an experience that perhaps goes back to Robert Flaherty's *Nanook of the North* in 1922. Nor need the person necessarily be central to the film: occasionally someone stands out vividly in the background, glimpsed briefly but never forgotten.

Every maker of a portrait film faces the question of how the film can possibly present its subject in any complete way. It is clear that, like a photograph, it can present a person's physical appearance, including details that might escape notice in everyday life. Films have an advantage over photographs, however, in being able to show the person repeatedly and in varied situations, engaged in a range of activities. This leads to a more rounded view and creates a strong impression of reality, yet even in the best films there is often a sense of absence and of something monumental and unreachable about the person seen on the screen. There may also be a disconcerting inevitability about the person's appearance and behaviour, for the subject of a film can no more look other than how he or she looks than act fundamentally differently from how he or she is.

The problem of how to present a person's inner life and experience of the world is more complex than presenting their physical appearance. It can be approached in part through their own words and at another level through the tell-tale signs of their thoughts and feelings. A person in a film may, if they choose, reveal through speech a great deal about their ideas, feelings and what they have witnessed in their lives, but this is always subject to their powers of expression. Quite often there is a great deal they are unable to put into words and other matters that lie at the very margins of their understanding. There are still other matters that they are likely to misrepresent, both to themselves and to others.

Portrait films are full of interviews and, less often, informal exchanges more like conversations with the filmmaker. Even if a person's words are not spoken directly on screen, they are often used in a voice-over commentary. This technique has been adopted very effectively in portrait films, an early example being Roman Kroitor's *Paul Tomkowicz: Street-railway Switchman* (1954), about a Polish immigrant in Canada who, during the night, sweeps the freezing snow and mud from Winnipeg's streetcar tracks. Here the very limitations of the subject's utterances and command of English become powerful metaphors for his life.

Apart from using speech, filmmakers can chart their subjects' emotional lives by observing their responses to the events and people around them. These responses may include both explicit expressions of feeling and the more general play of their emotions when engaging with others or with the filmmaker. How viewers interpret these signs depends on their acuity and background, but also on how familiar they have become with the subject's culture and personality through the film. As a film progresses, viewers become increasingly attuned to the meanings underlying the subject's reactions. At first they may interpret this behaviour according to some general typology, but with familiarity more subtleties begin to emerge. A smile given in one situation possibly indicates amusement or friendship but in another merely politeness or ironic forbearance. Identifying these responses correctly tends to deepen the viewer's identification and sense of complicity with the person filmed.

Jean Rouch often claimed that people are more likely to speak honestly when they are being recorded than when they are not.[3] One can understand that this might be true from the subject wanting to satisfy the filmmaker's wishes, or because the filming brings forth a desire to set the historical record straight. There is also often a confessional quality to interviews, as if the subject were stimulated by the occasion to say things they had been unable to express before. Being filmed seems to allow their minds to roam freely and explore thoughts not yet fully articulated. At other times the filmmaker's evident interest in them seems to stimulate their powers of analysis as they strive to explain some complex aspect of their personal life or social circumstances. There is something both confessional and analytical in the words spoken quietly by Maasai women to Melissa Llewelyn-Davies in her film *The Women's Olamal* (1984). Although these are matters that Maasai women might well discuss among themselves privately, the situation is altered by the presence of a sympathetic outsider intent on finding out how their society works. The women clearly respond to this both as an intellectual challenge and as a sign of friendship.

Filming of this kind can also provide an avenue for complaint. Sometimes the complaint is motivated by self-justification or the hope that it will effect a change. At other times it seems more to be a means of putting problems at an objective distance, to better understand them and perhaps be reconciled to them. A person's sense of powerlessness or confusion may be alleviated in a symbolic way by the power of words. The surge of autobiographical films made since the 1980s, such as Ross McElwee's *Sherman's March* (1985) and Tomer Heymann's *I Shot My Love* (2009), can often be ascribed to filmmakers using their films to confront and contend with problems in their own lives.

When we observe a person on film speaking confidentially to the filmmaker and then interacting with others, we often have an uncanny sense of being both inside and outside them: outside their social life but with privileged access to their feelings. We have the impression of sharing their consciousness, much like what we feel when we read the experiences of fictional characters in novels. In this way, films bring together two of the primary channels through which they address us, the public and the private, forcing us to reconcile what we see of a person's behaviour with what we feel we have come to know about them.

At another level a film can reveal something about a person through the filmmaker's own responses to them. These are encoded both in the types of scenes that are filmed and in how the camera is used to film them – whether there is a sense of intimacy, attraction, aversion or sympathy. The filmmaker, as intermediary, passes on these responses to the viewer, either consciously or unconsciously. Viewers interpret the way the camera frames the subject, how close it comes, what details it chooses, how it moves between subjects, where it lingers and so on. In this way the person's existence becomes embodied in the film partly by way of the filmmaker's own body. One demonstration of this can be found in the filmmaker's original decision to make the film. What drew the filmmaker to the subject? How is the subject positioned in the film? A complex set of attitudes emerges through the relationship that develops between them. In a film that touches us, we are drawn to the filmmaker's sensibility, and we participate in the filmmaker's interests, discoveries and pleasures.

Filmmakers sometimes feel overwhelmed by the sheer scale of the person they are filming, amplified by the knowledge that this is but one person out of millions, each of whom possesses a similar depth and complexity. They may, at the same time, feel a proprietorial pride and excitement at being able to bring the person to others. Some have compared this emotional state to spirit possession, or to being put in a trance, or even falling in love.[4] The writer James Agee described it as a yearning to put the 'cruel radiance of what is' into words.[5] And yet, for all the exhilaration it may bring, filmmakers often experience a sobering sense of inadequacy in trying to make a few scenes stand for the immensity of a life.

The Making of a Portrait Film

I have experienced a number of these feelings when making films, but perhaps never more than when trying to portray children on film. Why this should be so is unclear, but it may be a response to the openness of children's personalities or the memory of having been a child myself. I suspect it also has to do with being in the presence of minds and bodies still in formation, as children try out new thoughts and new ways of being. The urgency of their searching reaches out to the filmmaker, and often to the viewer. Some of their attempts clearly reflect their immediate culture and surroundings, but others have often struck me as more exploratory and, indeed, pre-cultural. This openness has tended to influence my own thoughts and feelings at the time of filming. In my encounters with children I have often felt changed into a more stripped-down version of myself, less structured and more receptive.

This state of mind became familiar to me while making a series of films at Doon School in Dehradun, India. The project had been suggested to me by an anthropologist who had studied three elite schools in northern India and was in the process of writing his PhD thesis about them.[6] Among the schools he had studied was Doon School, perhaps the best-known and most prestigious boys' boarding school in the whole country, with a tradition oddly combining the aspirations of India's independence leaders with the rigid conventions of a British public school.[7]

Within the first few months of arriving at the school I began work on a film about its ideology, rituals and structure. Not long after, I started another film on the experiences of boys in their first year at the school. This focused on 30 twelve-year-old boys in Foot House, one of the school's 'holding' houses for newcomers, named after Doon School's first headmaster, A. E. Foot. The life of students in Foot House subsequently became a major focus of the project.

I quickly found myself filming children both in the mass and as individuals. This double focus never posed a particular problem for me, although it did produce different filming strategies and different kinds of filmed material. What I most recall of the boys *en masse* was the impact of their physical presence: the chorus of their voices, the jostling, the thicket of arms and legs, the smell of skin and hair, the roughness of school uniforms – sensations familiar to anyone who has worked with similar groups of children. Other impressions included the sounds of running, doors opening and closing, names and imprecations shouted out and the tap-tapping of table tennis being played on the veranda. What I recall of the boys as individuals, however, was very different and was closely allied to the challenges of conveying their distinctive personalities on film.

I began as an observer, immersed in the midst of activities in the house, my presence tolerated but equally often ignored. After their initial curiosity, the boys began to regard me less as a filmmaker and more as another adult, although one who, as an outsider, had less influence over their lives than the school staff. I never directed them to do anything for the film nor interfered with their activities, and they soon lost interest in the filming. What might have intrigued adults about what I was doing was of far less interest to them than their immediate social needs and concerns. Because I was almost constantly present with the camera, they seemed to regard my filming as more or less neutral, emphasising no one thing more than any other. Several of them told me later that they remembered me clearly but couldn't remember actually being filmed.

I sensed this general indifference when filming group activities, but when I was filming just one or two boys a different dynamic often took over. Boys would address me directly, or show me things. Although I was an outsider, I was one with whom they could share certain activities: eating a meal, appreciating a joke, observing how other boys behaved. My curiosity was not in fact so different from their own curiosity about each other and the situation in which they found themselves.

For me their foreignness as individuals and as members of Indian society was a constant source of interest and wonder. The great differences in their personalities also soon became apparent. I tried to imagine their lives with their families, an upbringing so different from my own. I wondered how it felt to live in a child's body, which I only remembered vaguely from the past. Above all, what was it like to be a new person in the world, trying to understand its divisions of power and purpose?

While I observed the children and filmed them, they looked back at me with varying degrees of interest. Some made efforts to be friendly; others couldn't have cared less about me. How in the end my presence affected them was hard to gauge. For my part, however, these experiences were both vivid and unsettling. I sensed everything with a heightened intensity, and in this sensory overload there was both pain and pleasure. It was exhilarating to feel connected to their lives but frustrating when I felt clumsy and out of step with them.

The scope of my filming at Doon School gradually narrowed, moving from the first general film to films about two successive groups of boys in Foot House, and then to one final film, a portrait of a single boy in the second group. I first noticed him as I filmed his cohort arriving on their first day at the school. Most were accompanied by their parents, who were helping them carry their trunks and suitcases into the dormitories. I filmed the boys' faces as they inspected the new world where they would now be living. One face caught my attention. It belonged to a small boy, quite neat in appearance, with carefully combed hair and watchful eyes. What struck me most was his calmness, despite his obvious wonder at being in a new place. He did not have the stunned look of the other boys, who were glancing around anxiously. His was a more studied curiosity as he assessed his surroundings. Later I learned two facts that helped explain this. The first was that he was not from India but from Nepal. The second was that, unlike most of the other boys, he was already familiar with boarding schools, having been in one since the age of six.

He also had another quality, a special alertness or acuity that made him stand out. While looking at old photographs, my wife and I used to play a game as we viewed photographs of school groups.

As we scanned the rows of faces, we would often ask each other which among them we would ideally choose as our own child. Invariably we picked the same one. In such a photograph I would probably have picked this boy.

As the group settled into the house and I began filming them, I learned that the boy's name was Abhishek. On the first evening they lined up to receive their towels and school uniforms for the next day. As Abhishek's turn came, he turned slightly and looked back at me, at once acknowledging the filming (for the others seemed largely oblivious of it) and with a slight smile suggesting he found the whole proceedings amusing. His look seemed to say, 'We two are outsiders observing all this.' During the following days his interest in the filming continued, along with his slightly ironic view of school life. Most of the time he accepted being filmed along with the others, but there were other times when he looked directly into the camera and made a joke about it or some further sign to me.

For the next four days, because it was a mid-term break, the entire school went on a series of expeditions. The new boys from Foot House went to stay at an old Forestry Department rest house at Lachhiwala, where they were able to swim in a river and walk in the forest. I accompanied them on this trip and could see several friendships forming immediately as boys looked to one another for reassurance and companionship. Other boys, including Abhishek, joined in the general activities but kept more to themselves. I noticed, however, that he had a playful sense of humour, suddenly breaking into unexpected laughter at some joke or minor incident. I noted in my journal: 'He is rather solitary, often preferring his own company to that of the other boys, and yet he is not unsociable with them, nor does anyone seem to dislike him. But he is more intellectual and better educated than the others and tends to gravitate to adults.'[8]

One afternoon, most of us were resting on mats on the lawn outside the Forestry bungalow. Abhishek, who knew me a little by now, put his mat down beside me. For the next hour he talked about books he had read, films he had seen, and how he had attended a Jesuit boarding school in Kathmandu. He had definite ideas about knowledge and education. Later I noted: 'It's not only that he is precocious that makes him attractive – that could as easily produce a stuck-up bore – but that he has such cheerfulness and such a sense of wondering discovery.' Thereafter he continued to seek me out. Once I found him alone and asked him what he was doing. He said: 'Oh, I am just sitting here thinking of so many things, sir.'[9]

Back at Doon School, academic life took over again and I filmed the boys preparing for their classes. As I filmed these activities I would often discover Abhishek following me about. He enjoyed talking and joking with me. At one point he made me turn my camera in a full circle as he described what he thought it was seeing. For several weeks I filmed him and the others in Foot House intensively.

I was busy during this period trying to film the group as a whole and identify some of the individuals within it. I wanted to show how they were adapting to their new environment and how they were learning, in a very short time, the things they would have to know about the school. There were many episodes of confusion and awkwardness as the boys got to know one another. There were fights. There was homesickness. One boy began to be bullied. Abhishek always stood a little apart, although he got on well with the others. He joked with them when he felt like it, but without feeling obliged to join in. He seemed to prefer talking to the adults around him, which included me, the housemaster, the housemaster's wife (the house mistress), and a woman who served as the house tutor and counsellor.[10]

One day, as it was a holiday, there were no classes. The dormitory was quiet and I found Abhishek lying on his bed. I sat on the bed next to his and left the camera running, wondering what he would say to me. He began talking casually, and in this conversation, which I recorded in full, he seemed relaxed and even slightly drowsy. At intervals he would sit up and then lie down again, cease speaking, or speak reflectively as different thoughts came to him. It took only an occasional remark on my part to keep the conversation going. He spoke of wanting to be a scientist, of his success at academic subjects and of writing letters to his family and friends. This led him to speak of the dangers of going to the post office in Kathmandu, especially for children, whom he referred to as 'small people'. In an offhand way he remarked that children could easily be kidnapped for ransom or to harvest their kidneys, which could then be used for transplants, leaving the child half dead. There was something so shocking and coolly adult about these observations that I was left with a new impression of him. Here was a breadth of understanding I had not seen before, and a highly individual intelligence.

In the coming weeks I got to know more of Abhishek's nature. He could be sociable, but also at times dismissive of those he thought less intellectual or knowledgeable than himself. He read books more difficult than those read by his classmates. He found many things amusing, and when he was struck by some quirk or absurdity his laughter was infectious. Once I found him playing pranks on an older student, apparently in the hope of gaining his attention. He was interested in history, even though he proclaimed it his worst subject, and he spoke of the advanced technology of the Indus Valley civilization and Nepal's resistance to British colonialism, while at the same time deploring the country's lack of economic development. He was interested in language and the meaning of words, and he quickly improved his grasp of Hindi, which had been quite limited when he arrived. He was sensitive to the beauty of the school's campus, or professed to be. He could think quite analytically, perhaps influenced by his Jesuit teachers, and he was able to draw out general principles from his personal experience. He believed people should learn things for themselves rather than accepting the views of others. He spoke of the importance of family life and the need to recognise the feelings and situations of other people, especially those less fortunate than himself. Sometimes it seemed that he was repeating things he had heard before, but for the most part he appeared to be formulating his own ideas and exploring his own thoughts as they came to him.

It was these conversations with Abhishek that gradually led me to think of making a film about him. Until now I had planned only to include him as one of the boys in the general film about Foot House. I realised, however, that the conversations I had filmed with him would not fit well into it, for they were much too long and complex, and to use only brief fragments of them would both be awkward and fail to do justice to Abhishek himself. I nevertheless continued my filming of him for its own sake, for I felt there were few extended records of how children actually thought and spoke. Material like this might help to counter the often prevalent belief that children lack the perceptual and intellectual skills of adults.

In this way I slowly began putting together a film portrait of Abhishek. It eventually emerged as *The Age of Reason* (2004), its title referring indirectly to British Enlightenment views on childhood and to the age at which I believe children are capable of serious reflection and judgement. As well as recording further conversations with Abhishek, I filmed everyday events in his life and his gradual adaptation to the school, which was not always smooth. He spent some time in the school hospital with viral fever. One boy taunted him for his Nepali accent. With great effort he taught himself how to swim in the school pool. Throughout the first term he continued to be something of an outsider and to take refuge in his relationships with adults, especially with me and the house counsellor. It was only towards the end that he finally made his break from us. I felt this as a personal loss, for I had grown fond of him, but I also believed it was a necessary step for him to take. In this way the film also came to an end.

Over the next few years I maintained some contact with Abhishek. I saw him on my occasional visits to the school. Four years after the filming, I asked him to view the material I had shot of him, and whether he thought I should try to make a film out of it. He agreed, and a year later, when he was seventeen, I showed him the edited film, which he accepted with his usual humour and good grace. After that I saw him only a few times as he progressed through university and graduate work overseas, studying English, Irish and American literature. We exchanged letters every now and then. His were always cordial and detailed, describing his work, his thoughts and his current situation. As he completed his doctoral thesis he asked me to read drafts of it, which I did. I made very few suggestions, for here was Abhishek, meticulous to the last, exploring his subject with far more logic and precision than I could ever muster. Eventually he returned to India to teach at a new university. Somehow, for all that had changed, the connection between us held.

In Retrospect

The experience of making the portrait of Abhishek brought home to me the level of personal engagement required when trying to convey the being of another person, especially someone very different from oneself. As filmmakers draw closer to their subject a certain tension often develops, and perhaps on both sides a recognition that there is a boundary not to be crossed. In my filming of Abhishek I was conscious of taking a risk, for to do so was to commit myself to a process with unpredictable consequences. Despite the apparent rapport between us, there were also formidable differences of age, culture, experience and social convention. How close could I come to presenting him in his own existence and singular view of the world? What would the process be like for me, and how might it affect him?

There was also a suggestion of danger, for I was unsure how this interest in a child who was not my own might be interpreted by others. And yet to bridge the gap between us might be possible on some level. There was also the attraction of Abhishek himself and my wish to convey to others just what he was like. It was an opportunity I felt I should not let go out of fear or expediency.

In a portrait film, the relation between the maker and subject requires an interest on both their parts. The maker perceives something of value in the subject and tries to preserve it in the film. The subject responds to the maker's interest but also tends to look to them for reassurance. They may wonder what it is in themselves that deserves such attention. The filming may merely arouse their curiosity or it may create an atmosphere of complicity. There is often a kind of bargain struck, the subject giving something of themselves in exchange for the attention they receive. But this opening of the self, this vulnerability, is also reciprocated, for the maker too gives up something by acknowledging a dependence on the subject. The portrait is shaped by the relationship that develops between them. It is not a definitive drawing, but more often a series of impressions, propositions and tentative forays into the mystery of another human being.

At Doon School I was a foreigner, not of that place. There is something both inviting and unsettling about being in such a liminal position, disconnected from one's normal life but with one's perceptions and senses preternaturally alive. By voluntarily choosing such a state one performs an act of self-dislocation, relinquishing a degree of security. It is the same in one's contacts with the people one meets. Their very difference, with its unknown potential, becomes part of the attraction and part of the risk. Things may go well or badly.

One small incident brought home to me the distance between Abhishek and me, despite the things that had brought us together. I had just filmed him having his hair cut by the school barber, a taciturn man who made the rounds from house to house, cutting the hair of all the boys who needed it. The barber whisked away the cloth from around Abhishek's neck and Abhishek stood up. Quite automatically, without looking at the barber, he held out his hand, and the barber proceeded to trim his nails with a sharp knife. This unconscious gesture, with its innocent expectation that another would perform the task, pierced me with a sense of Abhishek's other life. For a moment he seemed alien and unreachable.

 I was a foreigner at the school, with all the uncertainty and dissociation that came with it. Abhishek was one too, so we had that much in common. It was perhaps natural that he should gravitate towards those in a position like his own. One of his few school friends was a boy from Bhutan. But for all the times that he seemed self-assured and even overconfident, there were also those when he seemed unsure and out of place. At one point in the film he wanders alone through the school's natural history museum, inspecting a skeleton, a snake, a human brain and a human foetus in a jar. Mixed with my absorption in filming this was also the question of what we were both doing there, which perhaps he wondered as well. It seemed as if we were on the edge of some precipice. Towards the end of the film he plays with a still camera I have lent him and takes a photograph of me. We face each other in an uncomfortable void, where time seems to have stopped. There is a sense that we have now seen altogether too much of each other.

—

1 See V. S. Ramchandran, *The Tell-Tale Brain: A Neuroscientist's Quest for What Makes Us Human* (Noida: Random House India, 2010), and Pascal Molenberghs, Ross Cunnington and Jason B. Mattingley, 'Brain Regions with Mirror Properties: A Meta-Analysis of 125 Human fMRI Studies', *Neuroscience and Biobehavioral Reviews*, 36/1 (2012), pp. 341–49, for example, on mirror neurons.
2 My own acquaintance with making portrait films was as follows. As a student I had made a short film, *J. Lee Thompson: Director* (1967), a study of the British film director;

and later, with Judith MacDougall, *Lorang's Way* (1979), a portrait of a Turkana elder in East Africa. Two other films could be described as 'triple' portraits: *Three Horsemen* (1982), also co-directed with Judith, about Australian Aboriginal stockmen in Cape York, and *Tempus de Baristas* (1993), about mountain shepherds in Sardinia.

3 In conversation, but also see James Blue, 'Jean Rouch in Conversation with James Blue', *Film Comment*, 4/2–3 (1967), p. 84.

4 In describing his state of mind when filming an initiation ritual among the Sorko people of Niger, Jean Rouch writes: 'I myself was in a sort of trance that I call a ciné-trance, the creative state, which allowed me to follow very closely the person who was being initiated.' Jean Rouch, *Ciné-Ethnography*, ed. and trans. Steven Feld (Minneapolis, MN: University of Minnesota Press, 2003), p. 183. When making *Los niños abandonados* (1975), about Colombian street children, Danny Lyon said he 'fell in love' with his subjects.

5 Agee expressed the purpose of his and Walker Evans's book *Now Let Us Praise Famous Men* as an 'effort to perceive simply the cruel radiance of what is'. James Agee and Walker Evans, *Now Let Us Praise Famous Men*, 2nd edn (Boston, MA: Houghton Mifflin, 1960), p. 11.

6 This was Sanjay Srivastava and resulted in his book *Constructing Post-Colonial India: National Character and the Doon School* (London and New York: Routledge, 1998).

7 I have written in detail about the school's origins and distinctive culture in *The Corporeal Image: Film, Ethnography, and the Senses* (Princeton, NJ: Princeton University Press, 2006), Chapters 5 and 6.

8 Journal entry of 3–7 April 1998.

9 Journal entry of 3–7 April 1998.

10 The Foot House tutor and counsellor was Minakshi Basu. She appears in a number of the Doon School films.

ALL THESE SUMMERS
—
THERESE HENNINGSEN

Second Life

I created an avatar in Second Life when it first came out. I was in front of a landscape, couldn't see anyone else in there and had hardly walked ten steps before I stumbled and fell into a puddle, face down. I couldn't figure out how to get back up. I made some committed attempts, but then lost concentration and left myself there. Two years later, I suddenly remembered how I had neglected my other self and logged back in. I was still lying there, in the puddle. Six years later, the same disquiet emerged, and I was back looking for my other, other self, since the email address I had previously used to log in had expired. I had accidentally taken all my clothes off and couldn't work out how to put them back on. It felt a bit odd to arrive at a party like that, but then it also seemed that many others were wearing more or less accidental outfits.

You've Got Something I Want and I've Got Something You Want

They had to get off at Sainsbury's but didn't press the stop button on time. They pressed it repeatedly until the next stop; I had to get off there too. We lived in South Africa most of our lives, they said, but moved to England in 1965. I added and subtracted, measured the curves of two almost identical faces.

I'm not sure why I invited myself for tea.

It would be our pleasure.
When would it be best to come?

Do you want coffee or tea?
Tea, please.

You don't drink coffee?
Sometimes.

We just have to wait for it to draw, he says.
Patience ... I suggest.
Yes. Patience. All good comes to he who waits.
He stirs, staring into the cup. I always wait. Nothing ever comes my way.

Two large velvet armchairs face each other and a small electrical heater. Parked below the heater are two pairs of slippers.

He points at the pictures on the wall. That's my nephew, he's a millionaire. That's my sister's husband, he's a millionaire. That's my other nephew, he's a millionaire. And that's my cousin, she's a millionaire ... They never tell me how they get their money.

Would it perhaps be okay for me to bring a camera?

There's no hesitation.

Of course.

Look, look, I made this. He shows me some bent metal, a bike accessory perhaps. I'm not just a pretty face. Motorbikes are parked for the winter. France, Germany, Belgium, Italy, Egypt, East London, South Africa, England, Spain, Isle of Man. I've been everywhere. I've been riding motorbikes since I was fourteen, and still ride them.

Come on, let's go upstairs. We return to the great chairs. PG Tips. Initial enthusiasm fades. Put that camera down. Your tea isn't very hot, so you better have it. I realise my access had less to do with the camera than my return.

As we sit, wrinkled hands gesture 'come sit on my lap'.

On one return, it's an early morning. I'm very tired and not entirely certain why I am embarking on a journey at this time of day. My shoulder aches from the weight of the camera box.

He pulls the door open as I knock, only slightly. You're here early. Do you want a cup of tea? He stands opposite me as I fiddle with the camera in the hallway. Blue and white striped pyjamas, long sleeves, long legs. There is something awkward about this motionless posture.

He pulls down his trousers.

You've got something I want, and I've got something you want.

… Don't do that, you know that's not why I'm here.

He bends down and pulls them back up. Oh yes, I suppose.

We stare at each other, silently, clumsily, both apparently hesitant in deciding what comes next.

I stay. We enter the living room and sink into the armchairs. He lifts his cup. You know, just because we get older, it doesn't mean we stop wanting those things.

There's a gentleness to the way he says it.

Sleepwalking

I met him on the estate in Seven Sisters where I live one afternoon. He was with his dog Olive, a Dutch shepherd. That morning, to temporarily relieve my inclination, I had been searching Gumtree for puppies and for rescue dogs at www.dogsblog.com. We talked about dogs. He likes to draw dogs. He has always had a dog, since he was in his twenties. He is now fifty-six. Having a dog makes him feel safer. More grounded.

When he lost his last dog, in his grief, he started growling at people.

He tells me how he rarely sleeps at night. His patterns are different. I tell him that I often wake in the night and am unable to go back to sleep. Perhaps we could go for a walk together at 4am? I would like to film our walk at 4am.

We meet on the ground floor of our estate. Olive is vigilant. He is also alert. He had untreated ear infections as a child, and later had to have surgery, so he is now deaf in one ear. His deafness makes his sense of direction unstable; he needs to use his other senses. He turns around, looks over his shoulder and spins back again. He says spatial awareness is important. You never know who you will encounter and what their intentions might be.

We walk next to each other. Slowly he lifts one foot after the other. Olive zigzags in front. He tells me that he likes to amble, and that I walk too fast. I bring out my camera, so my gait turns less brisk. There's an awkwardness to having a conversation and filming at the same time. Particularly when walking. I turn sideways slightly, pointing my camera to the left, speeding up a little in order to walk one or two steps in front. I'm unable to see my steps, so I end up lagging behind. Every now and then I glance at the street and run a few steps to keep up.

We walk along the canal. He tells me he was born in London, but his parents are from Cyprus. He hasn't been to Cyprus for a long time, but he lived there for seven years in his twenties. He dreams about Cyprus; that is where he feels he belongs. There's a sickness to London. When in Cyprus he would suddenly start missing London, especially the bird song. There are different kinds of birds here. He even started missing the sirens.

We cross a footbridge to Walthamstow Marshes. It's still dark; we glimpse six rabbits running across the field.

He stops and looks towards something in the distance.

You see that man over there? Does he have a dog? I'm just wondering what he's doing, why he's there at this time of day.

I think it's a woman?

I zoom in with my camera, the lens revealing that he is right. A man is sitting on the edge of a wooden bridge.

I think he's waiting for the sunrise. Look, the sun is just about touching his face.

Struck by his acute awareness of his surroundings and those occupying it, I notice my own inattention to people's possible ill-will.

I ask him if he's sometimes worried that he might be ... I'm not saying that you are, I'm just wondering if ... paranoid?

Conscious, he says ... or maybe there's a term that's stronger than conscious but less strong than paranoid?

We don't manage to work out a suitable term.

On the way back he tells me he wants to show me something. We walk around the corner of a red brick wall on our estate. In a small space behind the wall, I discover a temporary shrine. On a table, there is a framed picture of a woman, and flowers and cards. *In loving memory – Mum – I miss you so much.*

He asks me if I want a cup of tea, so I go with him to the fourth floor. We wait for the water to boil.

I like to help people who are down, he says. I like to pick them up. But sometimes you can't get your claws into them, it's too late, like the woman who jumped, I only spoke to her twice, and then she jumped. If I spoke a bit more, it may have stopped her from going that way, that's why I cried when she died, it hurt me. I actually spoke to her. It's sad, so horrible, there's no help for people with depression and things like that. Life becomes ... you're isolated until you die.

He walks over to the window and looks out. I read people's body language from here. Whether they're energised, not energised, on the march to work, you can tell what mode they're in, you can roughly make it out. I like that. Body language analyst. It's almost like people are ... sleepwalking.

During the time of restrictions, we meet regularly at 4am and walk. To the marshes, to Lordship Rec, to Springfield Park. Sometimes I film, sometimes I don't.

One day, when out for a walk, he strokes his right arm. When you're not there, I feel it in this side of my body. He tells me he feels different after having met me. He is uplifted and has started to look forward to things. Like when Olive does a swirl on the spot in excitement, he says. It sometimes feels like freefall and makes him feel exposed and vulnerable. He's used to being on his own and doesn't normally allow himself to trust people. My attention discombobulates him. He looks the word up on Google as I mention one day that I had felt discombobulated after a nightmare. I say that I learnt this word when I first arrived in London, and since then it had often felt appropriate. We laugh and repeat it to ourselves several times. Dis-com-bo-bu-late.

Later, as I review footage of one of our conversations, I notice how he seems more articulate than me in his reflections on our encounter. I repeat myself and only manage half-sentences. When you meet other people, when you meet people ...

I stumble, partly because I don't know how to respond, and partly because I'm simultaneously holding a camera, aware of both frame and focus.

I start to speak. It's also about ... it's also about ...

He assists me in the completion: ... You. It's also about you.

All These Summers

It feels like climbing Alpe d'Huez on a three-wheeled bike, he says. He likes to think of apt metaphors to humour whoever happens to be in his immediate vicinity.

His face then turns solemn, and he looks at me. It's hard work, Therese.

I'm here on my first visit, witnessing his gradual yet rapid decline.

*

I wake up. He usually rises before dawn, but there is no sign of him yet. It is still dark. I walk up the stairs to his room with the camera in my hand. As I enter, he is sitting at the edge of the bed, staring into the floor. It's happening, he says. That's what it is. I think the depression is coming back.

You can feel it?

I don't know what's what.

I hesitate. I want to reassure him, but there is a recognisable air of imminent transition, so I'm not sure how.

Do you want a coffee?

Together, we go to the kitchen. He sits down and continues staring into the floor.

I tell him that I recently read a short article referencing Harold Pinter, who apparently once said that when writers stop taking the bus, they lose the ability to observe, or habit of observing, the lives of other people.

I always liked to observe people, he says, but now even the smallest impression overwhelms me.

I suggest we read a little. Perhaps I can read something out loud? He is hesitant but agrees, if it is a small paragraph. I find a short section from Jon Bang Carlsen's book *Inventing Reality*, which I have just picked up from the post office. I bought the only copy I could find online a few weeks back, but the antiquarian had misplaced it, and it took him a week to locate it. I imagined him searching the shelves of the bookshop for the missing item.

To show doubt is not a sign of weakness, but a sign that the person is not petrified in a preconceived view of life.

Stop, he directs.

Doubt was always important to me, he tells me. I kept telling that to other people. I would say to them: Doubt is a blessing. You can do one thing, or you can do the other, who knows what's right? He has had enough of the reading by now. He gets up, walks a few steps, then stops in the middle of the room and stands there, still. He looks at me with a kind of hopeless sadness, endearing almost, like he's looking for something but not sure what or where to look. I smile at him and laugh a little. Don't laugh, he pleads.

He looks out through the window. There's a discrepancy between what's happening in my body and how beautiful it is, he says. He opens the door and starts walking around on the grass outside. I observe him from inside the kitchen. I get an urge to film his directionless wandering and feel a sense of affiliation. I start to wonder why I feel an affinity now that he is suffering. After a while, he comes back in and asks: Can I make a monastery in my own home? What do people do when they go to a monastery?

Oh, I don't know, they pray?

They breathe.

I now must learn to be in the pause, he says, between actions.

I just don't know how.

He takes off his glasses and polishes them. He tells me he's been trying to imagine a big subterranean parking lot: when the bad thoughts arrive, he will say hello, welcome, now please go to C3 and park there.

He mutters an ominous repetition as he continues his aimless roam.

I can't anymore.

I can't anymore.

I can't anymore.

*

We are sitting in the waiting room at the hospital waiting for his radiotherapy treatment. Two women are sitting at a table in front of us. Mother and daughter. They discuss whether the daughter should go to Norway for Christmas.

>It's ok for me.
>I'm not sure Jørgen would agree.
>Why not?
>You know, he's so traditional. Also, we don't know how long granddad has left.
>I would quite like a trip to Flensburg, we could drive across the border.
>I was thinking of a trip to London. There's a Diana exhibition at Kensington Palace I want to go to. I've said to myself, next time you go, you make it a goal for yourself to queue for the Diana

exhibition, however long it takes. When we go to Copenhagen we should only do two things, remember that. Tivoli and La Glace, we only do two things and go home. There's a Wakeup hotel next to the station, they have a family room, two rooms with a door between.
But I don't have a back-ache anymore.

I can't stand listening to them, he says.

Why?

Everything becomes a reminder of others' aptitude for life.

Tuning in to other people's conversations has been a shared trait of ours. To the extent that we sometimes forget to listen to the one we're in. Habitually turning our heads to study the faces connected to the voices.

It reminds me of a sentence from Annie Ernaux's *Exteriors*, where she describes looking at a woman in the Métro and thinking: Why am I not *that* woman?

Stop staring.

Sometimes, I say to him, I'm perplexed at the certainty of people's convictions.

We don't know very much about anything, he responds.

I fly back to London. In the airport, my bag is taken off the belt to be searched. Something showed on the monitor, though I had already taken out the usual culprits: computer, hard drive, camera. A woman searches the bag, finds the object and turns her head, holding it up, triumphantly. She shouts back to the woman who is standing at the monitor: Look Lise, it's just a cheese, it's just a cheese. Look Lise, it's a cheese.

Not long after, I need to return. He has a room on the eighth floor of the hospital.

He asks me what I have been doing. I know so little, he says, and maybe I won't be able to understand or cope with new thoughts.

I tell him that Andrea and I did a workshop on clumsiness in filmmaking: 'Clumsy Encounters'. I used the description of the ethnographer and writer Michel Leiris' cultivation of a *methodological clumsiness; a permanent inability to fit*. The actual quote says 'methodical clumsiness', which in my mind had turned into a 'methodological' one. He doesn't listen. I'm not surprised. I begin deciphering the difference between the two.

Give me a quotation, I teasingly demand. He hesitates, then looks up: Life is not for beginners. But that's not yours, that already exists, I object. Does it? he asks, but he's distracted, waiting for the nurses to arrive. When the hell are they coming?

The nurse finally comes in. Good morning, she says.

Outside his window there's construction work. They are expanding the hospital. He shudders at the noise of the machines. It's crazy to think about what the world is doing, he says, those sounds, I guess you could interpret them as positive sounds. It is strange how one's mind can do somersaults.

Two crows fly by in the sky, screaming. His eyes follow their journey; I think they're laughing at me. You deserve it, they cry.

What are you afraid of? I ask.

Dying, he says. I'm afraid of being a burden to you. A burden to others. I'm afraid of not becoming myself again.

Who is 'yourself'?

That's the big question, who am 'I'? He pauses as he considers the question. I get completely dizzy at the thought, he says.

I sit at the edge of his bed. He's staring into the ceiling. I squeeze his hand. He holds on to mine. I'm scared now that you are leaving.

As I land in London, I receive a text message from him.

All these summers.

On the train back from the airport I repeat these three words to myself as I stare at the passing landscape. His regret for the unrealised. Repetition of a season, non-linearly, divided by the other seasons. My mourning, again, of an absence in his presence, like the fifteen, sixteen and seventeen summers ago.

—

With gratitude to Trevor, Raymond, Pete and my father for welcoming me and my camera into their lives.

THE LENS AS SHELTER
—
MARC ISAACS

IN CONVERSATION WITH
THERESE HENNINGSEN

Interview conducted in Markfield Park, London, on the occasion of the release of Isaacs' film *The Filmmaker's House* (2020).

THERESE HENNINGSEN: How did your interest in hospitality come about and what does it mean to you?

MARC ISAACS: I'm trying to think when I first started thinking about hospitality. I don't remember the moment it came into my mind as an idea, but obviously at some point I committed to making a film where people were going to come into my house. I read Derrida's book *Of Hospitality*, and I watched lectures on YouTube because I was interested in people interpreting it. One of them was Anne Dufourmantelle – is that her name? You told me about her and suggested a book I should read about gentleness. Is that right?

TH: *The Power of Gentleness.*

MI: And I read that. I discovered she lectured on Derridean hospitality specifically, and there are ideas in there that struck a chord with what I was doing, especially regarding the figure of the homeless person; I'd already cast a homeless man, Mikel, to be in *The Filmmaker's House*. I also saw a talk about Islam and Islamic hospitality: the idea of being offered food and shelter for three days and three nights. And, meanwhile, I'd already cast my Muslim neighbour.

I also remember reading, and I think this is Anne Dufourmantelle, talking about the figure of the mother and the womb as a site of 'ultimate' hospitality – a home that you provide for your yet-to-be-born child. That got me thinking about Lacanian psychoanalysis: the idea that you're thrust out into the world and then life is about trying to recover something, you experience a kind of otherness. Otherness would have been in my thoughts anyway, like with my other films. So yes, it was an interesting discovery and some of this theoretical stuff found its way into the film in a very direct way.

For example, I gave Mikel lines for a scene where he is talking about his mother: 'I came out of my mother's womb and all my problems started. 'Another example is Nery losing her mother and not being able to go to her funeral; that's a real story that happened some years before. So the word *hospitality* in a way came in and gave me another way to look at what I was already doing, because of course I was very aware of the fact that I was inviting these people into my home. I was aware it would be not only about my relationship with them but also their relationship with each other and, in the film, what the possibilities of that are and what can be played out in a 'dramatic' way.

TH: There are many things here that relate to the theme of hospitality. Derrida says: 'To offer hospitality … is it necessary to start from the certain existence of a dwelling or is it rather only starting from the dislocation of the shelterless, the homeless, that the authenticity of hospitality can open up? Perhaps only the one who endures the experience of being deprived of a home can offer hospitality.'

MI: Yes, and I think when I read that myself I was also aware of the hierarchy in these relationships, both between me and the people I cast, and between them. For example in relation to Mikel: the fact that he doesn't have anything to offer. Nery provides a service, and the builder is there to do the fence, but Mikel has nothing. So we tried to think about how to give him agency. He refuses to talk about some things, and when I ask him how he ended up like this while he's in the bath, he says: 'You'll never know me. You can never know me.'

Then we thought about the actual camera itself in terms of hospitality, about what the filmmaker has to offer. When you film somebody, you have control or a power over them, but you also offer your subjects – horrible word – something. You listen and you give them a space to reveal things that are important to them.

TH: It's interesting because hospitality has an air of openness but it also necessarily entails a power relationship.

MI: Yes, and Derrida spoke about the fact that there's no such thing as *absolute* hospitality, because there's always a power relationship with something and the risk that it involves. You have to take a risk. I quite like that idea in the film, in that it's a risky thing to do, to open up your house in that way. It's not a fiction in that sense; it's my house, it's where I live. Mikel walks past every day, and he still does now. My neighbour is still my neighbour, and Nery is looking after my children this afternoon. So I'm working with people who are still very much in my life, which feels quite a risky thing to do in some ways.

It was interesting to think about that: what are the limits of hospitality?

TH: Derrida also talks about the distinction between *conditional* and *unconditional* hospitality, between the Law of Hospitality, and laws (in the plural) of hospitality, where unconditional hospitality requires giving place to the absolute, unknown, and anonymous Other, asking neither reciprocity nor their name. How does this unconditional hospitality relate to your work, and what becomes possible in the encounter if we take this notion of unconditional hospitality as a guiding principle, the utopian ideal of this unconditional welcome?

MI: What interests me is that utopia inherently implies that there's some other life somewhere; it implies a perfection, which is a bit scary. I think when I started making films I was much more subconsciously utopian than I am now. Now, especially with *The Filmmaker's House*, it's much more about the act of inviting people in and exploring these themes, rather than saying, 'Oh, wouldn't it be lovely, we can all live together.' It's looking at how life is, not how I want life to be or how I think life could be. It's about how things are. In a sense, it creates a very artificial situation because people don't come across each other in real life in the way they do in the film. But for me that's what's interesting, that's what film should do. It's impossible to film real life; you create something to make you think about these things – that's kind of a big lie, but if you look at it the other way it magnifies some truths.

I found it interesting to read about the limits, or the conditional and unconditional aspects, of hospitality. For instance, in the film, I'm not sure at what point we even know Mikel's name. I was very aware that we should keep holding it back, that he shouldn't introduce himself in that way. That we shouldn't label him, in a sense. He says at some point that he comes from Slovakia, and I was aware that we should play with that a little bit. It's really important that there were conditions on hospitality, both in terms of the story and because I just don't see how one could be unconditionally hospitable. As soon as you meet somebody, you're weighing them up: who are they? What do they want? There's a power dynamic at play straight away that you can't rid yourself of because of social context.

TH: We're always informed by where we come from, and how we see …

MI: … and I love it when I get surprised by someone who I build up to be one thing and they become something completely different. It's always interesting, isn't it? Makes you feel a bit stupid.

TH: What do you hope to achieve by bringing different and disparate people together? Particularly in relation to the dinner scene in *The Filmmaker's House*. Or perhaps you don't hope to achieve anything?

MI: I don't actually hope to achieve anything other than some human moments. There's no idea behind what the film can achieve. Well, there is an idea: the idea is to explore all the awkward, interesting things that I see that could happen in that encounter – people's ideas, people's prejudices, their aggression and also their kindness – the range of human emotions and thoughts that the situation can offer. You might not like somebody's food, but it doesn't mean you don't like them. You might be disgusted by something another person does; how do you hide that or what do you show of that? You may be able to really empathise with somebody when they tell you they've lost their mother, yet you've been aggressive to them moments earlier. I love the fact that people are different. If there's anything to be achieved, it's to celebrate that difference and not judge it.

I get very uptight about a lot of aspects of political correctness, because I think it can be really dangerous. It can impose a uniformity on things that is totally unrealistic. What was interesting about making this film, in relation to that question, is that Keith has some really appalling views about stuff. I remember one of the assistants who was working with me would come to me afterwards and say, 'I really don't like that', and get very judgemental about him. I understand that, because they were really awful views, but as a person I'm much more accepting that he has those views and that's his problem. If he suddenly got aggressive and violent, then I would think completely differently about it, but I also think it's important not to just stay in your own little bubble of people who have the same view of life as yourself. People need to experience each other.

TH: I was thinking about that phrase Anne Dufourmantelle references where she talks about going towards the edges of what we know and this idea of 'the opening onto what disturbs' [Derrida quoting

Patocka], which I felt drawn to, because it feels like maybe what we believe to be true is not always …

MI: Yes. I think I'm a very simple person. When I see somebody like Keith, I imagine his history. I don't know the specific details of his history, but I see a guy that got through school, started working, lived in his community; he's a Londoner, uneducated, but a decent, warm-hearted guy who was very generous with me. But he can have some views that are wrong, and these are a product of his time and circumstance. And that doesn't make him a terrible person. I think if you go around pointing fingers then you'll get what you want: an angry bunch of people on the streets, disempowered, with no stake in the world that they live in. I think that's extremely dangerous.

I pretty much believe that people should say what they want and we should argue with them, debate with them, rather than ban people from saying stuff. And yes, it will offend people, but then you have to shout back at them. [*Laughs*]

TH: Tell me about the biblical story of Lot and his daughters that you refer to in *The Filmmaker's House*. Can you first tell the story briefly, then talk about how you interpret it and how it enters into the film?

MI: That came about because I was thinking about Islamic hospitality. The making of *The Filmmaker's House* had a very different dynamic to films I've made in the past. The film is, on one level, rooted in my inability to get funding to make it. So I thought: how do I show my character in some way? I never had any intention of making one of those American films where the filmmaker is turning the camera on himself in a very obvious and direct way, but I did start thinking about who *I* was. At one point my parents gave me some old photographs, from the beginning of photography, of my family, and they look like Hasidic Jews and Roma: Eastern European peasants, basically. I put them up on the mantelpiece and I arranged it so that the characters would notice them, to produce a moment in that scene. We filmed this but it didn't fit in the end.

When I first moved into the house, I had a conversation with Zara, the neighbour's mother-in-law. When we caught each other in the front garden, she said, 'Are you moving in? Are you Jews?' She actually said that, and I included it in the film, I thought it was very funny. It's the kind of thing my grandmother would say, as a Jewish grandmother, to somebody else. Very direct and blunt. I said to Zara, 'I'm just human', and we started laughing. I would never take offence at that remark. Even if it was antisemitic, it would wash over me. So I thought, that should be in the film in some way.

And then, to go back to hospitality, I started thinking: well, what about Jewish hospitality? What does it say in the Old Testament about hospitality? There's the story of Lot. Strangers arrive at Lot's door and he offers his daughters to the strangers. It's a really dark, horrible story, and I decided that I should use that and ask Zara to ask me, 'Well what do Jews do? This is what we do in Islam, what do Jews do?' And I tell her that story about Lot offering his daughters to the strangers.

TH: Can you talk a bit more about Nery's role in the film?

MI: It's hard to talk about what the beginning of the particular idea for this film was, but I started to think about doing a film in quite a different way from what I'd done before. At one point I invented a film that was again going to be with real people, set in an Essex seaside town with white people who had gone to shut themselves away. Then I was thinking about making a film set on 29 March, the date the UK was going to leave the EU; that was an early idea. I was also intrigued by how I could work with people I know, or people who are local to me. I thought for years about filming my neighbour, and even filming Nery, but without any frame, without any idea, just because I'm always thinking, 'Oh, that could be interesting for a film' when I meet people, and Nery was part of that, too. *The Filmmaker's House* has its roots in all these ideas.

I decided that Nery would be one of the characters, and then I had to think about what she would do, and I felt that the story with her mum was really interesting. I remember when it happened, because we actually lent her money to go home, and she did miss her mother's death when she was flying back. I think her role is ... I don't know what her role is, really. I know what I wanted to explore with her: this sense of being away from home, not being able to go to your mother's funeral, and the sort of mystery to why she doesn't want to go back. To explore her sense of where her attachment is; where does she root herself, where is she?

When I cast these characters to be in the film, then the questions came up: what is their role, what's their position, what can they do?

TH: There's also something nice about this moment when she asks you, 'What should I do in this situation?' You're working out between you what to do in this situation you've created. It feels very moving somehow.

MI: It's also very much how I work more broadly. I'll decide something and then think, I've decided this now, what can I do that's going to be interesting? I decide that I'm going to set a film in the house and these are going to be the characters. It's not the other way around; it's not taking a notion, an idea that I plucked out of thin air, and then finding everybody to play those characters. It's what's going on in my life: how can I use that?

TH: We've talked before about risk and tension in your filmmaking process. Why are those elements important to you?

MI: For me, every film has to have tension. The things that I'm interested in exploring have some dramatic quality to them, because it's people's emotions, their struggles. I always try to think about what the emotional heart of something is, and it feels important to me that if I'm going to have a person in my film, they reveal something of themselves, emotionally ... their humanity. So there's the characters themselves and then, in my films, there's a kind of tension around something to do with the world we're living in now. But it's secondary, it's a kind of backdrop to what's going on. In *Men of the City* [2009], the backdrop will be the City. I didn't know in that film that the financial crisis was going to impinge on the film, and I actually didn't like it when it did so much because the whole film suddenly became about that. So I had to rethink and use that in a more timeless way, not getting into the details of the financial crash.

So it's the two things: it's the characters' stories, their loneliness, joys, tragedies, but also within a certain social context, something that feels like it's asking questions about the world we're living in, in a subtle way.

TH: How do you see it as being a reflection of you? You're not turning the camera towards yourself, but do you encounter yourself through filming others?

MI: It's a good question, and one that I think has changed over time. In the beginning, the films changed me more, in a way – they had a direct effect on me and my thoughts – but each one is different, depending also on the process of making it. When I made the film in Calais [*Calais: The Last Border*, 2003], the actual experience of being there and making the film became quite interlinked, just because I was going there a lot and I was away from home and I was living there while I was making the film. Whereas if I'm making a film in London, and going home every day, it becomes a very different experience. But on an emotional level, when you film, things really touch you, and if the film flies around a bit afterwards and you encounter it in different places it kind of ... I never sit and watch my own films, but I will watch the odd screening at a festival if I'm in the mood, and even if I don't watch it, I'm encountering it again and again, because people ask me about it, or I'll do a Q&A. There's always a deep effect that it has on you; it doesn't leave you, it stays with you, but it's hard to measure. It's a constant exploration.

There's a strange kind of split that goes on when filming other people: you're looking through the camera and you're filming these moments that resonate, and they're often painful for people – they're talking about difficult aspects of their lives – yet the glass of the viewfinder and the lens is a sort of shelter. Sometimes, you're so into the moment, the cinematic moment, that you forget that it was real. There's a split that happens, and when something goes wrong, it's like the lens gets smashed and reality creeps through and smacks you round the face. I think that's interesting because it's something that's always a possibility in documentary films, on different levels. And the fact that these people are all in my house: it's exploring that they not only come into my house, but they come into my camera as well. Adam Ganz, the writer, pointed out that *camera obscura*, the Latin, means 'room'. It's interesting that the camera is the room. As filmmakers we tell stories. We're still telling a story of somebody, and you're always walking this line of what's possible and how is it going to affect people. It's not without consideration, but you don't really know. Every film is a different experience.

TH: I also want to come back to this idea of what we imagine to be possible and under what circumstances, and that of course comes into *The Filmmaker's House* with the whole framework of not being funded.

MI: It had a massive impact, yes. I wouldn't have been able to sell this idea at all. I've always taken risks, but now things are so homogeneous in the industry. I'm stubborn and I want to be free to do what I want to do. If the funders don't come with me, then I'll do it another way.

TH: Because to get funding you have to define things under certain ways of seeing and doing, it feels like those frameworks only allow for the shape to be already formulated.

MI: Yes, it's predetermined. I love the discovery, you know? An idea: dive in, swim out with something interesting or dare to foul, dare to take a risk and dare to screw up. There's no room for that really in the mainstream; as soon as you take serious money from people, you're in a prison.

TH: That also comes into *The Filmmaker's House*, not being able to film ordinary people.

MI: It's a bit provocative in the film, because what the hell is an ordinary person? But there is something real about it in the sense that the industry likes the extraordinary and I've always filmed with ordinary, everyday people. So I play around with that notion in the film: what is ordinary? I'm so not interested in a sensational story *because* it's a sensational story. There are some great films that deal with sensationalist subjects in a good way – I'm not saying that it can't be interesting – but it's never really appealed to me.

I think it's to do with the fact that I see filmmaking as a way of life, so I want it to connect to my life. My life isn't full of murder and dead pop stars. I want to make things that are relevant to me and my life, which are human feelings that we have inside us every day – they're not extraordinary. I think it makes life much more bearable, somehow. When I watch a simple film that's just quiet and films that I can return to again and again, they make me feel better about life. Whereas if I watch a film about a serial killer, I don't feel better about life at all. It's hard to describe, but I want films to have a quality to them that gives you a breath of fresh air, some energy.

TH: There's something in that that I feel drawn to as well, and also the tragicomic, which we talked about before in relation to Chekhov's short stories, which felt informing because this is part of life. There's something very beautiful …

MI: … it's beautiful, yeah. It's not that it's good or bad or whatever, it can be beautiful. That's what I'm striving for. I know that I'm never going to feel content in life. I might feel slightly more content than I do now, at some point, and I try to feel more accepting of what this thing is and try to reduce the anxiety.

Sometimes when I finish stuff and I look back at it, I'm like, 'Oh, that's how it turned out.' What I like is when it raises more questions than it answers. I look back at *The Filmmaker's House* now and I like the fact that there are questions that aren't easily answerable about the form, about the people, about how it was made.

TH: Films asking questions rather than providing answers.

MI: I don't like certainty very much. You and I have never lived in more uncertain times, and it's bloody hard to wake up every day thinking; you can't really actually think more than a week ahead without everything being extremely complicated. And that's interesting, because we create all this certainty and it's just illusory, isn't it? We all know that we can get run over and die tomorrow, yet we make plans for next year. I don't like chaos, and I need some certainty in my life, but the uncertainty, the unresolved things in films, are interesting because we're all unresolved, we will be until the day we die. I never believe it when people say they're happy in their life, I think they're lying. Maybe there are some people who wake up feeling happy. I don't understand.

STRANGERHOOD: ON THE ART OF OLIVER BANCROFT

—

GARETH EVANS

> A man's work is nothing but this slow trek to rediscover, through the detours of art, those two or three great and simple images in whose presence his heart first opened.
> — Albert Camus, 'Between Yes and No'

> A place is an idea, an idea is for a while a place.
> — Jorie Graham, 'Time Frame'

An Apology

This text does not seek to describe or explain Oliver Bancroft's enigmatic, moving and often profound paintings (which can be viewed as wished and indicated below). Neither does it seek to analyse the specifics of his painterly technique. Rather, through a series of notable 'portals', it considers certain strategies or positions – as the writer understands them, not seeking to claim they are how the artist views his process – in light of the broad thematic framework proposed by this volume.

For those who are interested to learn more and explore Bancroft's work further, a visit to his pages on the extensive and informative website of the Goldmark Gallery (as well as the extremely impressive operation itself *in situ*) is wholly encouraged (links below), as is purchase of Bancroft's 2021 catalogue *Somewhere Else*, very modestly priced, generous with its images and supported by a welcome essay from poet Hilary Davies, to whom this writer is grateful.

> *Stranger* (n.): late 14c., unknown person, foreigner, from Old French *estrangier* – 'foreigner'

Hamlet opens with the most primary of interpersonal interrogations: *Who's there?*

The response that comes does not furnish a name, but rather a retort: *Nay, answer me: stand, and unfold yourself.*

As audience members we do not know who is speaking, or to whom. As it's situated on the castle battlements at night, the location barely informs us of more. And yet the true enquiry is directed less to another, or between people, than to oneself, as the titular protagonist will demonstrate at considerable length in the acts that follow. Two words that contain such multiplicities: readings both external and deeply interior.

Those among us who are fortunate to know Oliver Bancroft can attest that his figure is distinctive. Extremely tall, his hair worn long, he smiles both vigorously and often. He is generous and kind and knows that kin matters, matters greatly, but not only or exclusively; knows that one makes one's own kin through active declaration of an often unspoken but always deeply held solidarity of purpose and perception.

When he is able to stand up from his powered wheelchair, it is most usually with the assistance of two thick wooden sticks, more substantial than canes, branches almost. He has multiple sclerosis, an inherited condition, and has been living with it for some years now. However, rather than yield to the reclusion its effects might provoke, he ventures widely and regularly across London and beyond from his flat in Greenwich, deploying the transport network to his firm advantage for gallery and cinema viewings, social meetings, landscape discoveries and more: he is often keen to be 'somewhere else'.

This is mentioned so early because Bancroft himself does not conceal it. Indeed, in the catalogue to his 2021 exhibition, his gallerist Mike Goldmark mentions it in introductory comments on the first page; not as any kind of excuse or plea for indulgence, but rather to explain Bancroft's absence from exhibitions for the last decade (he has shown his films widely during this period). This information is not intended to define either Bancroft or his work to the viewer, and yet it is inevitable perhaps that it inflects our experience, just as it does – far, far, more – the artist's.

Illness, disease or living with chronic incursions, each and all remind us acutely that we are both absolutely ourselves, contained within the body, and another person – a being in pain – who threatens to overwhelm us, replace us. Daily life becomes navigation – and attempted maintenance – of the space between these two identities, seeking to ensure that the latter does not entirely shadow the former.

> *Within* (adv., prep.): Old English *wiðinnan*, literally 'against the inside'

Through no choice of his own, Bancroft in public is now identifiable as 'other'. He is forced into new 'relation' with the built, majority and individualised environment. He is both seen, as a wheelchair user, and also often formally 'unseen', ignored by systems, structures and a certain class of person, in the way that millions of marginalised people are, whether economically and socially or because of gender, ethnicity, disability, belief or orientation.

Mobility is, of course, not only physical. Travels in mind cannot be limited by the exclusionary practices imposed; but for Bancroft, whose entire aesthetic purpose is about manifesting vision, this enforced invisibility presents most likely a double challenge: to him as a person and as a maker. Where he 'sees' possibility and potentiality, he is presented with obscuring and obstruction. This, along with his own inherent creative compulsion and challenging turns in a number of life circumstances, has meant that he has had to draw on deep emotional – even existential – resources of spirit.

> *Document* (n.): early 15c., 'a doctrine'; late 15c., 'teaching, instruction' (senses now obsolete), from Old French *document*

(13c.), 'lesson, written evidence' and directly from Latin *documentum*, 'example, proof, lesson'

It is perhaps not surprising – although still remarkably fortuitous – that Mike Goldmark both admires and has supported Bancroft for many years: 'For me, he remains the best painter of his generation.' Goldmark's own situation – for decades well away from metropolitan centres and transport hubs in the market town of Uppingham, Rutland – has meant that he has had both to work that much harder for traffic and sales (in earlier years) but also that he has become extremely clear about what he wants to do, and promote, and why. This rigour of attention, and intention, finds its mirror, perhaps inevitably, in the practice of the artists to whom he is drawn.

Encounter (v.): *c.*1300, 'to meet as an adversary', from Old French *encontre*, 'a meeting; a fight; opportunity' (12c.). Weakened sense of 'meet casually or unexpectedly' first recorded in English early 16c.

In 2005, the year of his first exhibition at Goldmark, Bancroft also showed in another solo show marking the end of a residency in Marlborough, helpfully named 'Life should be full of strangeness – like a rich painting'. The title, from a lyric in a song by The Fall called 'How I Wrote Elastic Man', appears straightforward but immediately begs extrapolation. So it is with many of Bancroft's images.

There is a broad and recurrent template: a terrain of usually open ground and sky (horizon lines are clear and median), an indeterminate site normally without human structural imposition, occasionally given extra arboreal feature, on or within or against which a mostly single subject exists: a standing figure, an animal, a tree or trees (there are significant exceptions to this, which shall be addressed).

Flora and fauna are central to Bancroft's inherently democratic, species-just, non-hierarchical and ecological sensibility. Donkeys, bears, dolphins, lions and birds: the tenderness with which they are revealed bridges and briefly defeats the gulf of otherness. In *Mouth Piece*, a man wearing broad braces – as Bancroft does – places his arm around a bear that appears to be contained. In *A Lion*, two human figures meet and touch brow to brow *inside* the creature.

He is especially drawn to the first named – perennial beast of burden, stoic, still, enduring. We think of Robert Bresson's *Au Hasard Balthazar* and Béla Tarr's *The Turin Horse*: *in a storm, in the eye of a storm, frightened by lightning, after the storm* ... It is only in the latter canvas that the creature is in motion, but free at last, Muybridge-light, off the ground and at full gallop, running from/to ...? In pale conversation with the cumulus above, it is the movement that matters here, the dynamic of change, just as the cloud itself is constantly in flux ... The nurturing impulse is apparent here, but never monotone. Look at *Donkey Suit 1.0* for an example of a genuinely distinctive take on what solidarity might mean.

At the other pole, Bancroft's solitary figures appear resolutely fixed. They make up the most immediately recognisable grouping in the 2021 exhibition, although they do not all belong to the same series. There is an ongoing sequence called *Holiday Snaps* ('Red Legs, Figure 1'; 'Beach Coals, Hot Sky'; 'The Sun'; 'Night Lights', and others). Such paintings *seem* to deliver more or less what their titles identify but there is something at work within them that pushes realism – however defined (here, let's say a recognisable object, gesture or setting) – into an altogether different realm.

That's not to suggest they are easily symbolic or literalise a metaphor. They also resist direct allegory. Perhaps more accurately they might be called 'atmospheric'.

Often when reviewing more left-field world or art house cinema releases, underpowered critics who are struggling for handholds might

Donkey Suit 1.0

declare that the work is 'beautifully shot' or 'extremely atmospheric' – faint praise to conceal or deflect from huge deficiencies as they see it in the basic elements of what makes for satisfying film-going: narrative, pace, characterisation, psychology etc.

This is not at all what is meant here in relation to Bancroft's paintings. In his scenarios, atmosphere is not some varnish smeared on the surface to 'lift' or 'enhance'. Rather, like the planet's own atmosphere (without it we're dead, vacuum-packed in cosmic drift), it is intrinsic and fundamentally necessary. It is first the space within which his protagonists operate, enabling their frequently enigmatic manoeuvres. It also appears to be generated by, or certainly in collaboration *with*, them. Sometimes this is realised through brushstrokes or palette; at other times via *mise-en-scène*.

This process of atmospheric density *envisions* the situations depicted, heightening their suggestion without in any way appearing rhetorical. This might lean them towards the metaphysical or the melancholy, the insightful or the inscrutable. These are figures that act as lightning rods to zones of interior significance, the nature of which we can only guess at. Just as we can't see the wind, only what it affects, so implication like weather presses in.

Elsewhere, in standalone works, figures seem at ease in surroundings that might or might not be materially 'real': *River Walk* and *Walk in Water* display a levity of mood and colour, but is that a walking frame, or handlebars, in the foreground ... There are figures with canes. There's a person up to their thighs in a flaming cauldron (less here 'the fire that comes from the painting', the influent energy of making by concentration on the needs of the image itself – as he related to Hilary Davies – and surely more the flares of muscular and neural distress that rise and fall like tides).

Then there's the mysterious, even sinister, faceless figure of *Souvenirs*, with his case and oddly aged baby in arms. It feels like we're in Peckinpah's territory now, crossing troubled borders in night's hot, velvet arms.

But there's also communion, joyous communion to a beat. In *Dancing*, a couple is as close as can be under the lights; *Embrace* grants a smile-wide sweep of energy to blurred bodies, their desire dissolving them into their surroundings and each other. It is Baconesque in its painted proposal but celebratory, not predatory.

Is this a memory or a yearning? Whether or not, it is no less present or true for that. And for everyone, there's always a moment when the *Dance Floor* is empty. Bancroft's, however, blood red and open to the land, feels entirely self-sufficient. It could almost be an organ, pulsing gently in the savannah heat. Life takes many shapes.

Souvenirs

The palette for Bancroft is generally earthy, imbued with yellows and gold, inclining to stormy or clear in its sky-lights. As Davies has observed, and as noted here, there's a keen and hugely informed historical awareness in the painter's brush. Referents, influences, motifs, nods, homages, echoes, refrains: any and all, call them what you wish; they evidence an active and continuous dialogue with the variant lineages of the idea and scope of the image as it has manifested itself.

His sensibility places itself inside what it looks on, operating as a station on that journey of looking *and* an agent of use or

The Witness

departure, while acknowledging it is only a part. This is perhaps why trees are so significant in the work. Often definitive in terrain, framing and contextualising, charging encounter, they serve a number of purposes. Samuel Palmer's visionary copses are recalled in *Edge of the Yellow Field*, while kindred spirit William Blake could preside over – even straddle the branches of – *Magic Tree*.

And yet ... if so, why is there a body strewn at the base of the trunk, legs and torso severed from each other? Goya is stalking the solar circumference of the tree's canopy cast now. The arboreal is ambiguous. In *Witnesses*, a figure stands between two trees. Each casts effectively the same shadow. *The Witness* presents almost a twin of the precedent painting. Singular, plural – who's watching? What's watching? What have they seen?

Meanwhile, in *Securing the Orchard* the figure is more actively employed, roping down a trinity of trunks; but why, against what? The day appears benign, although the low hills framing the field perimeter are ink-dark, as if a storm cloud has fallen to earth and survived.

It's clear now that titles do all kinds of indicative labour, ranging widely across the spectrum from nominal to associative and then off into the provocatively suggestive, taking on much of the heavy lifting in terms of completing our audience with the image.

That's not to say Bancroft should be described as a writerly painter. This is embodied work, not cerebral but enquiringly intelligent and keen for connection. Which helps to explain his love of music (and considerable knowledge of its subcultural, vanguard, world and hybrid branches): the extraordinary Alabama-born self-taught assemblage artist, educator and improvisational singer-musician Lonnie Holley is a standout, guiding figure for him. Operating within and without a tradition simultaneously, Holley is framed only by the horizon, and often not even that. Modesty of resource, coupled with a restless creative ambition – a literal sense of creating *with* 'mother universe' – delineate a life salvaged from brutal early expediency and loss.

Pursuing the sonic, we might look to the space between planets with Kubrick's *2001* but be listening to Radiohead's deep breath of 'No Surprises' when we meet Bancroft's *Pilot 1* and *Pilot 2*. Let's stay with the band then, and switch to 'Pyramid Song' as we chance upon his own *Pyramid* ('I jumped in the river and what did I see? / All the things I used to see / All my lovers were there with me / All my past and futures… / There was nothing to fear and nothing to doubt / There was nothing to fear and nothing to doubt').

Certainly their allusively poetic sense of challenged presence, the accumulating disquiet and compromised but nevertheless

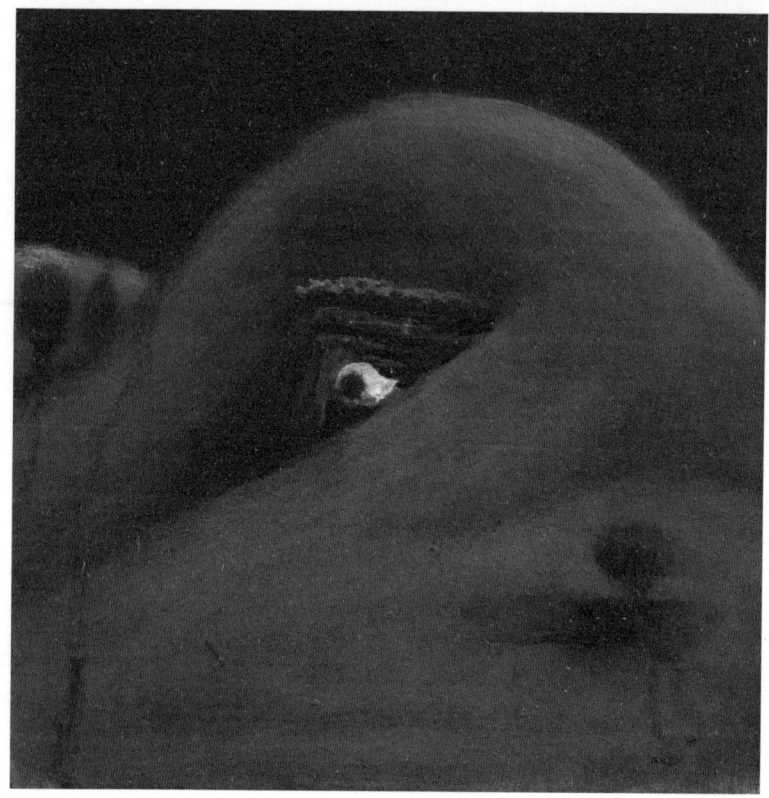

Eye of the Hill

compelling beauty feel like useful accompaniment when considering several of Bancroft's most mysterious images. Their titles alone could be lifted straight from one of the group's album track listings. *Eye of the Hill* and *Remote Wooden Wisdom* speak to each other while remaining resolutely themselves, and both hark back to an ancient pre-modern era of instinctual faith and pervading animism. Legend, myth and superstition; each wrestles, like music, with what is felt but which cannot be held.

The other medium of importance is film. Bancroft himself is a maker on 16mm as well as a cinephile. His is a tactile making, thinking frame by frame, with the camera as a mode of manual (as well as optical) extension in the manner of the brush. It privileges patience, precision and selectivity but still believes in urgency (to register the ephemeral).

In the scriptwriting and editing of narrative cinema, they say one should come into a scene as late as possible and leave as early. Painting as Bancroft practises it also draws from this. His could be said to be time-based too – indicating duration and narrative within the single fixed frame of the image (although his *Lions Feet* makes a witty play on filmic motion). Things are paused but not stopped. Questions therefore are raised: what happened before, what next? Suspense infuses the oils. We might almost think of it as 'suspended cinema', not an arrival but the capturing of a process under way; a step or station, a footprint on the path, evidence of being.

Film is a medium of place as well as time, of course. The thing filmed existed *somewhere* while it was shot. It takes time, in both senses. We cannot separate Bancroft's work from his sense of place, and that means firstly and finally his studio. An extremely simple, functional room that opens onto a high river wall in Woolwich, London, it is reached via a waterside route through some of the last remaining dockland warehouses yet to be fully gentrified. Just out of view by the shore, the half-submerged former Mersey Ferry *MV Royal Iris* lifts and drops on each tide like a collapsed lung briefly gasping into breath.

This stretch of the Thames (watercourse of both Conrad's half-lit *Heart of Darkness* and Blake's pastoral joy clear of charter) marks an approach to the threshold between river and estuary, where waters mingle and the city yields to its defining geography. It's uncertain, unpredictable, long overlooked and unconsidered by the Capital's central authorities. In this there is a lack, a poverty of opportunity and such, but also a wayward freedom. It feels several steps clear of complete surveillance. There's a non-judgemental generosity to local interactions. It makes sense that Bancroft has made his creative claim

Lions Feet

to such a location. The solastalgia increasingly felt globally is perhaps a little less established here currently.

And the riverrun pitch might also give us an insight into his compelling paintings *A Sail* and *A Rig*. Pictures of a masted (framed) canvas on, respectively, framed board and canvas, yes; but the masts stand in earth and nowhere is there water to be seen. Fixity and the longing to be away; a yearning that can no longer be realised: he has said, 'Let the picture tell you. You must leave yourself behind.'

Just as 'somewhere else' is not at the last a topographic position but rather an emotional, even philosophical compass reading, so Bancroft's oeuvre navigates between physical or material realities and the intangible but undeniable constellation of expressive needs realised in paint. Clearly an optimist, Bancroft is nevertheless beset by concern for the world and the trials of his own body. He knows both the *Oasis Pond* and the *Snake Pit*. Being in the world, he is painting the world he wants to, *can*, live in. He is under no illusions about what might come, which is not to say he refuses the pleasures of dream.

He is searching for a meeting with – and painting – the 'stranger' emerging from within him – his own future, as for all of us – and he paints this constantly repeating, elusive encounter in light of art's history and his own past; and in the colours of ochre, whisky and rust; the hues and tones of distilled and earned and felt experience, of living on the magnificent, mutilated earth.

This is singular but not insular making. Each brushstroke is a determined act of will – the mark, gesture and gift of a citizen of that territory most open and welcoming to all: imagination.

Now evening feathers our eyes. *Elsewhere* murmurs through the leaves. The donkey in the far field raises her head. The last of the light rests on her mane, but the myriad of stars reminds us we are not alone.

—

Full details of Oliver Bancroft's work (including many of the paintings referred to here) and exhibition can be found at: goldmarkart.com/oliver-bancroft/artist/oliver-bancroft. His mixed-media project *Birds from the Dark Parts of the Map* is forthcoming. Please contact Goldmark Gallery for further information.

Warm thanks to Mike Goldmark, his team at the gallery and, of course, to Oliver Bancroft.

GORDON'S FACE DEAL

MARY JIMÉNEZ
FREEMAN-MORRIS

Climbing the old stairs that lead me to my father's room, I see him at the top of the stairs looking at me and calling me Arturo!

Between us I hallucinate a beam of intense light. A light stronger than reality since my name is not Arturo. I am not his brother but his daughter, and my name is Mary.

That's the way my mind is set; that's what I believe.

Am I right?

He sees it differently. I am not his daughter; I am his brother, already dead many years ago.

I feel estranged, projected out of his life and mine and brought back as another.

Why would I believe I am right? What should we do with our alienated identities?

Is there such a thing as an identity? Don't I believe that life is in permanent mutation? Who projects what, goes hand in hand with the question of who loves whom, and in which way. How to welcome this name, which within my imaginary world is not my name?

I believe in images. I have seen truth so many times in a cinematographic frame. So many times, things I cannot see with my naked eyes appear when I see them framed.

I put a camera in front of our two faces and take a shared selfie; I ask him to look at us, and to tell me what our names are.

'My name is Lucho,' he says, 'and you are Arturo.'

I have no choice.

I welcome our new names over the pixels' inclemency. We become father and brother. I give hospitality to the other that I will become for him, and to the other him that he will become partly for me, and the making of a film begins.

Face deal.

I accept the face you give me and I take the other face of yours. I will be the girl I am and your dead brother. I abdicate and forsake my old identity and enter into your logic. I accept the deal because your love for me is there, untouched.

The film gives us hospitality, unites and separates us.

The deal eschews reason and welcomes mutual acceptance, however crazy.

Isn't it always like this every time we film another, who for the duration of a film agrees to be just a character, a small and sometimes foreign part of themselves? And who are we in that kind of deal? Which is the part of ourselves that seeks itself in these exchanges? Is this a hidden form of transformation that lies within the tissue of film production?

Identities carried away. Lost territories torn away from old and hollow magic carpets moving away in space and time.

You said your father had some business in Nova Scotia.
But aren't you my father?
The Japanese used to call it Nova Scotia.
Are you in Nova Scotia?
No.
But my father is? If my father is in Nova Scotia then you are not my father. Are you my father?
No. Not anymore.

—

The film *Face Deal* (2014) was made when my father/the father was 102 years old.

PRICK ME WITH YOUR CALAMITY, WIND ME WITH YOUR FAMILIARITY

—

ANDREW & EDEN KÖTTING

OFF WE GO AGAIN THEN – Cabin Doors to Manual
Diary entry 7 April 1988: Leila induced last night @ 54 cm
11.45pm – A baby girl was born – emergency caesarean section –
delivered by Doctor Fish – 8 lb 10 oz – food pumped directly into her
stomach – doctors concerned that baby is not behaving normally.
A year later.
A church step somewhere in the French Pyrenees.
Medieval.
Archival.
On a day so hot I was worried that the top of her head might burn off.
Eden, a daughter.
Eden, a catalyst for my new beginning.
Life before Eden and life after Eden.
What was to become of me? Us?
Her Joubert syndrome meant that she was missing a bit of her
cerebellum.
Her vermis. Some brains.
I'd finished at the university and the thing that is the wholeoflife was
in front of me. Us.
And this remembering like the urge to tongue a wobbly milk tooth.
Consuming. It takes me right back to when things are never that clear.
Not then.
Not now. They never were.
But
There it is. There you have it. In the picture. In the frame. Fairly full
to overflowing with the pain, of then, notknowing.
The philosophical, physiological, biological and historical pain
of notknowing.
Those elements, those autobiographical components that inform
the whole.
The corpus.

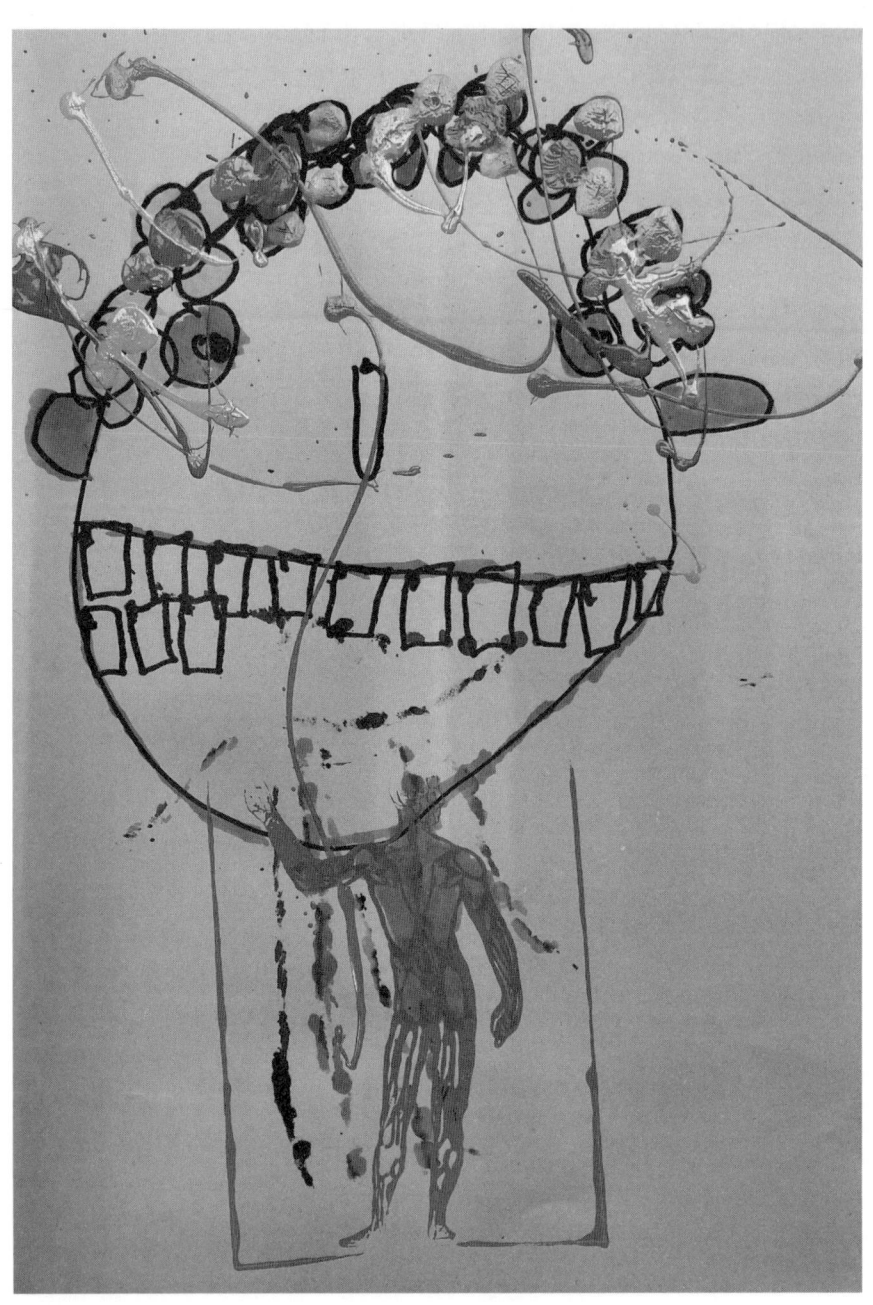

Her body.
My body.
The remembrances leap out at me again. Comes the ache, come to remind me of the heaviness of my step upon realising that the diagnosis for her condition meant that her life expectancy was not good. Was not long. She might soon be gone.
Dead and buried.
Thus
There she is. Was. Perched on the church steps. Barely two years old. Top girl on the top step, about to topple over. She leans into me and I kiss her. My kisses prevent her from falling. Falling back into the ambition and naïve determination to keep going.
Me, thus combatting the notknowing.
The photograph, mysterious and potent, rendered into the very fabric of my existence. The pebbledash of life.
What do I do?
I keep looking at my own life from different angles, keep trying to find new metaphors for the self and family.
Poetry from documentary.
Home movie from mundanity.
The keeptrying, the keeplooking, the keepremembering.
Memory, around which the self orbits.
B is for ... the beginning
B is for ... Body.

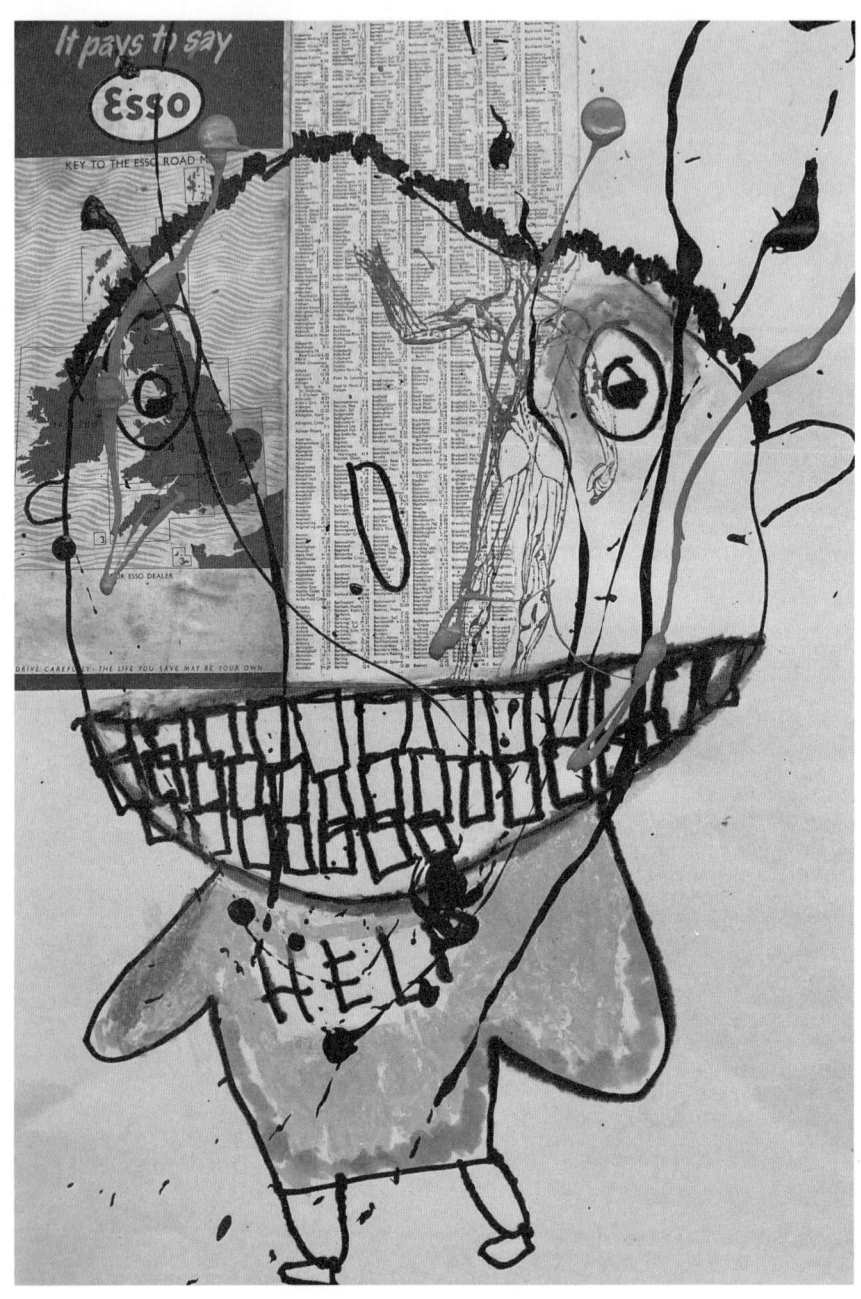

PRICK ME WITH YOUR CALAMITY, WIND ME WITH YOUR FAMILIARITY

Both vessel and votive, subjective and objective. B is for …
Being and the layered readings.
So
What does it mean to make work about oneself when herself has become myself?

The articulation of coherent intention when dealing with Eden (my daughter) can sometimes feel gratuitous and forced, and yet she ventriloquises me regularly.
Maybe she's doing it now.
Here I am in a garden shed in a light industrial unit on the Ponswood Estate, it's getting late and she's making me write this.
She is in me and around me.
She is unfathomable and frustrating, irritating and tiring, she is overwhelming and inspiring, life-stopping and life-enhancing.
She is an enigma and antidote to the dogma of religion and superstition.
She is real and not invented. She is needful every day of her life, from the minute she can't get herself up until the last thing at night when she can't put herself to bed.
Nothing is EVER taken for granted with her.
Nothing is ever assumed. Nothing is ever easy.
Her mother, my lover and partner Leila, and myself grab at moments in time – all the TIME we are with her. They are slippery and non-linear.

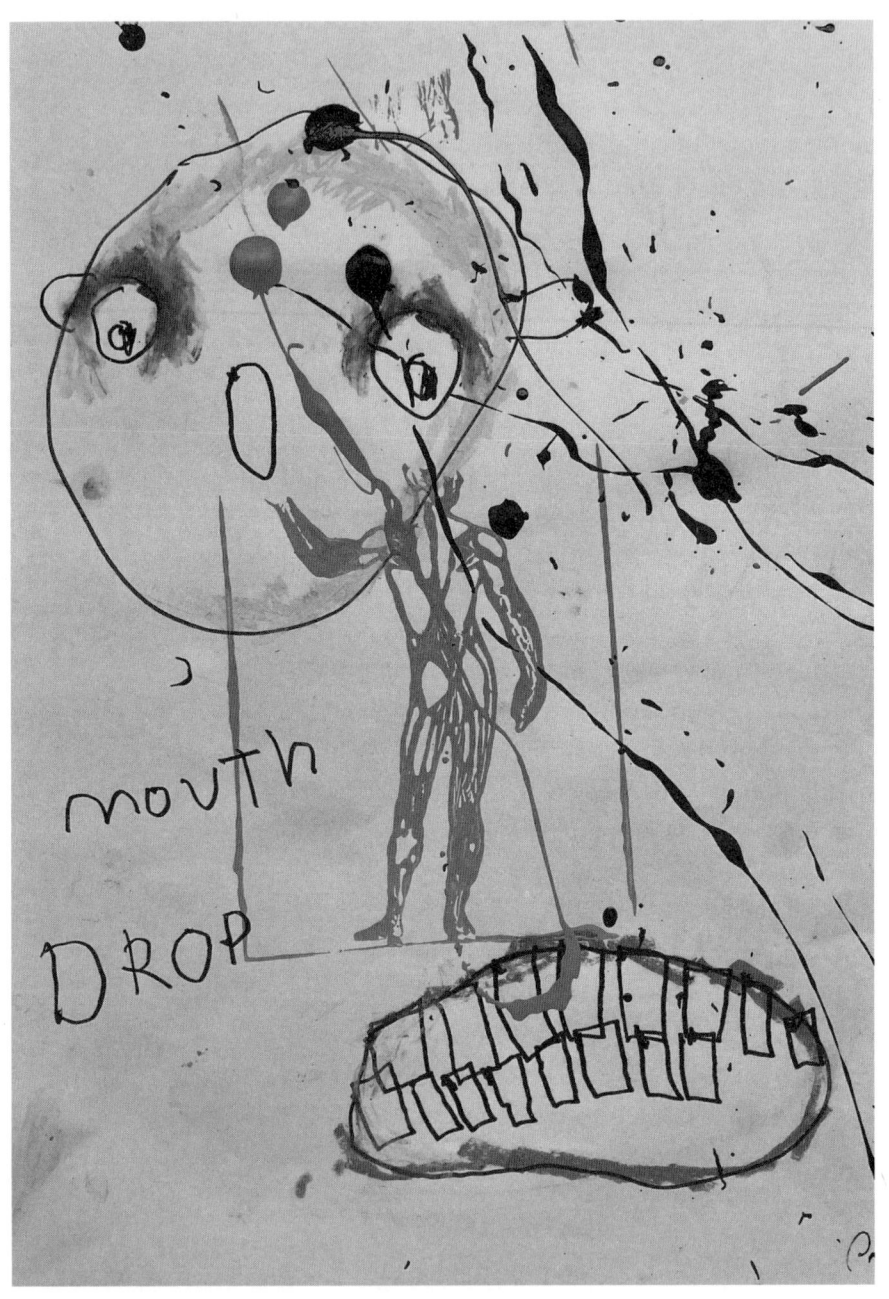

AND
As if that wasn't enough, there's the repetition, the looping, the
saying the same thing again and again and again – the saying of the
same thing again and again and again
What am I doing today daddy?
What's for breakfast daddy?
What are we going to do now daddy?
Can you tighten my bra please daddy?
Can you put on my trousers please daddy?
Undo my dress please daddy?
Can you pull my pants up please daddy?
What are we going to do now daddy?
Can I have some music please daddy?
What music is it daddy?
I'm hot I only want a T-shirt on today please daddy
(Even if it's snowing).
What am I doing today daddy?
What's for breakfast daddy?
My bra's too tight daddy.
Do I have to wear a bra today daddy?
Can you help undo my trousers please daddy?
What are we going to do now daddy?
Followed by, I'm happy happy happy
We are stuck in some Beckettian NIGHTMARE.
Repetition is a demonstration of the many becoming the one, with
the one never fully resolved because of the many that continue to
impinge upon it.
It is also very dangerous because it can drive you round the bend.
Resolution and conclusion are inherent in a plot-driven narrative.
However in real life there is no PLOT, we are hanging on by the seat of
our pants, waiting to see what might happen next.

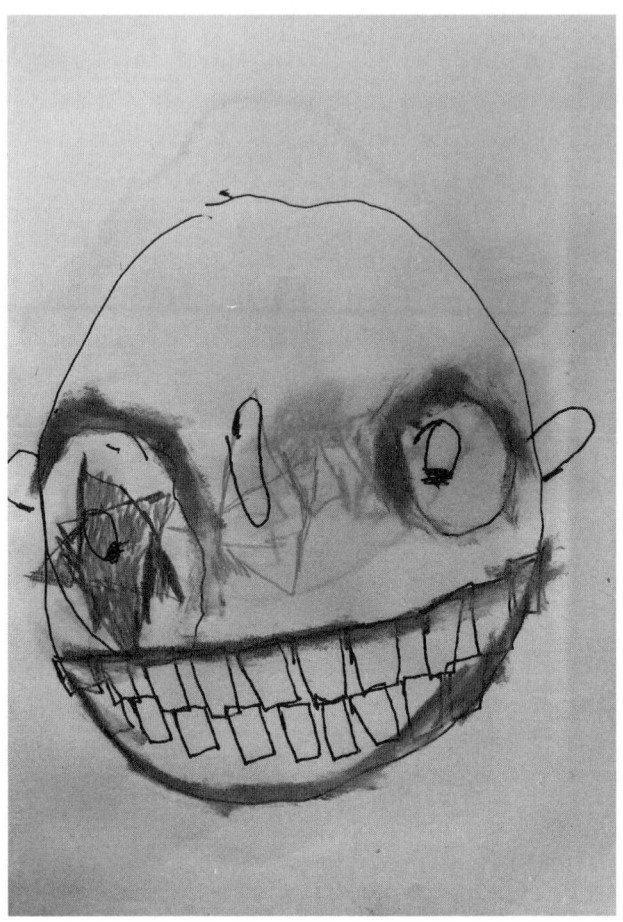

Thus since there was Eden there is no longer a history, just autobiography.
I draw heavily upon the nostalgia and fog of our own saga.
She draws heavily on collage that I have prepared for her.
There she is looking down on me now.
I make work about it.
The whole content of my being shrieks with contradiction when trying to discuss HER.

I love it. It makes me feel real. It makes me feel alone. Sometimes I have no idea what there is to say.
Nevertheless I MUST work with her in an attempt to placate my insanity.
I need her but not as much as she needs me. She is oblivious to the woes of the world, politics, economics and blight. I am the malcontent, not her.
Nonetheless – she is sensitive to mood swings and has ears like a bat's, she picks things up, she feels things and she is canny in her manipulation of US.
When I was younger I was full of hope that one day I might be able to glean what goes on in her head.

Consciously or unconsciously we deploy control over our memories to include or omit certain aspects of our lives.
Every documentary film, even the least self-referential, demonstrates in every frame that an artist's chief material is themselves.
It is an excavation of oneself.
Thus it's always difficult to separate what happened from what seemed to happen.
Memory is the past rewritten in the direction of feeling, and anything processed by memory is fiction. Therefore our memories are fictions.
Memory loves to go hunting – especially in the dark.
I'm interested in the generic edge – the thin membrane between what might be called fiction and non-fiction – but I draw from the real to make an 'unreal' or 'ethereal'.
She just draws.
Draws from life.
From me and my life.
Our life.
Our NOT still life.

ANDREW & EDEN KÖTTING

MY head used to be full of questions:
What does it mean to set another person in front of the camera?
Am I not trying to extract something from their soul?
When am I exploiting?
When am I exploring?
When am I adoring?
Is it one and the same?
Is it not impossible to do both?
Is it not the truth of human relationships?
She made me ask:
Will Eden live through puberty?
How will I deal with her menstruation?
Will she ever be able to form words that relate to her inner world, her inscape?
Will her mind ever be mined?

Today I return to the same question, again and again.
Will I ever truly know her?
Life is full of the stuff that flies at us in bright splinters.
It is full of cut-ups, blip-verts and misunderstandings.
It is a mosaic, deprived of wholes but FULL of parts.

228 PRICK ME WITH YOUR CALAMITY, WIND ME WITH YOUR FAMILIARITY

Everything I have ever made with Eden is a form of collage, it is just a matter of adjacent ideas and conflicting voices.
The trained and the untrained, the coherent and the incoherent.
This very writing is a pasting of ideas, an approximation of things that I'd like to say but don't have the wherewithal or plot to hang them on.
The altar of plot.
Perhaps plots are for dead people?
Knock knock – who's there?
Let the right one in?
Knock knock – who's there – cows – cows who?
No they don't they moo.

Collage is pieces of 'other' things.
Collage demands fragmented materials, often misaligned and even out of context. Collage is, in a way, an accentuated act of editing, picking through options and presenting a new configuration, albeit one that is never smooth and complete within the 'traditional' sense. The act of collaging might even prove the key to the post-postmodern predicament, it might even be the present-day nonbinary norm! AND the gaps between the paragraphs, the silence between the NOISE are equally as important.

The fish that never quite get to wherever it is that they are going.
This as an attempting-to-make rather than the finished product.
The getting-lost-en-route rather than the arrival.
Art is NOT truth.
Art is a lie that enables us to recognise truth.
Our art is a haphazard assemblage of some of these parts – the parts that seem to fit – maybe it ALL fits? Which is why I leave this BIT in.

Eden's SYNTAX is a tree-like structure, spreading out from a combination of limited root words and ideas that she tries to express. It grows very slowly. It's a shadow that hangs over me which is why she is back to ventriloquise me.

With her, all is contingent.
All is up for grabs and I'm left with a wonderful acceptance of all things being an approximation, always axial, never fixed, and this succours me.
It satisfies me.
It's a feeling that I have Eden to thank for.
If Eden wasn't interested in drawing and painting and collaging then I think I would have killed myself by now.
She is my therapy and I am her therapist.
We help each other.
We spend time together.
We make work together.
We blunder onwards together.
We live together.
We care for each other.

Monotheistic belief systems and their potential for fanatical misinterpretation at the hands of MEN frightens me.
It obsesses me and depresses me.
I worry about what becomes of her once they've done with me.
I seek solace in the lame excuse that the purpose of it all is to lay bare the questions hidden by the answers. Don't talk unless you can undermine the cacophony.
However no human being can exist for long without some sense of their own significance.
Worth is worthwhile and without it we are lost. So we grab at what's to hand.
Eden is always to hand.
I've been corrupted by the notknowing – it continues to feed my way of being.
The unfathomability of it all.
It is hard to march behind a flag of confusion and vagueness but behind it I march – immersed in the little stuff.
The quotidian.
The repetition of our life led.
We let THE BIG STUFF take care of itself.

PRICK ME WITH YOUR CALAMITY, WIND ME WITH YOUR FAMILIARITY

The marks that she makes I see as readymades, things that when repositioned or 'arranged' begin to take on a new meaning or importance.
A shapely swirl of energy holding shattered fragments together, but only just.
And in particular over the last five years we've started to introduce maxims or texts, which imply BIGGER significance or existential relevance.
They are the ideas that I'm pondering at the time and they relate directly to projects that I might be working on – and in this way the two become entwined and I have the patience to continue.
I'm hoping for new meaning, I'm reverse-engineering in an attempt to create PUNCTUM. If we're lucky it works and something pricks.
Is there anything intrepid in the artist's gesture of striking out towards the unknown, not only without a map but without certainty?
Is there anything of worth to be found?
Probably not BUT we keep doing it ...

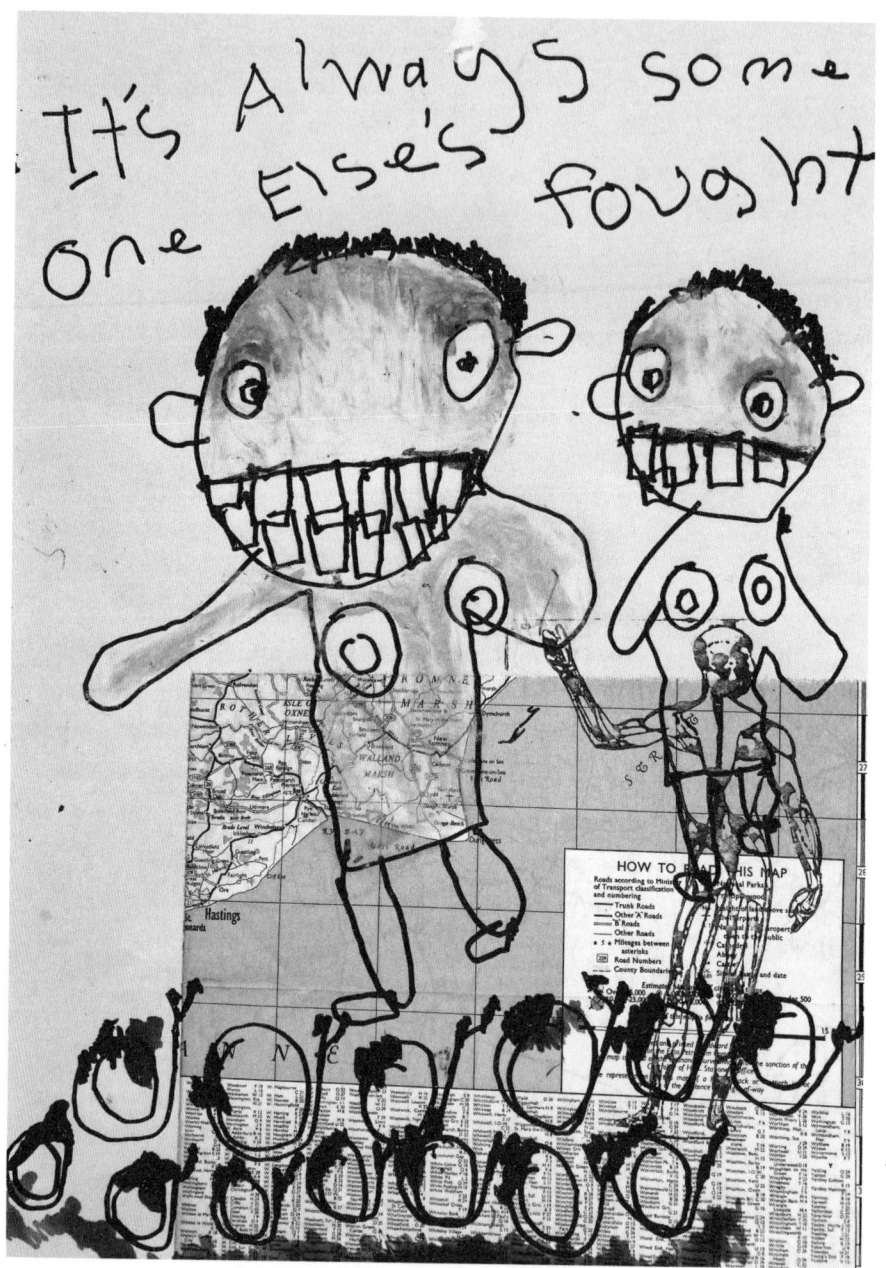

PRICK ME WITH YOUR CALAMITY, WIND ME WITH YOUR FAMILIARITY

When we are not sure we are truly alive.
Eden reminds me that I'm not sure most of the time and yet *she* makes me go on.
I blunder on.
I wouldn't be here today if there wasn't some grandiose idea within all the confusion that I had any notion at all of what I might be saying. She makes me do it and through the act of doing it
Intermittently
I feel as if I might be getting somewhere ...

I'll conclude now but not with a conclusion, there is never a conclusion, it is all ongoing, all spilling in and out of itself.
Perhaps nostalgia dressed up as the hauntological bride of implied memory.
Therefore:
The motor of fiction is narrative.
The motor of essay is thought.
The default of fiction is storytelling.
The default of essay is memoir.
Thus:
Fiction = no ideas but in the things themselves
Whereas
Essay = NOT the thing itself but ideas ABOUT things.

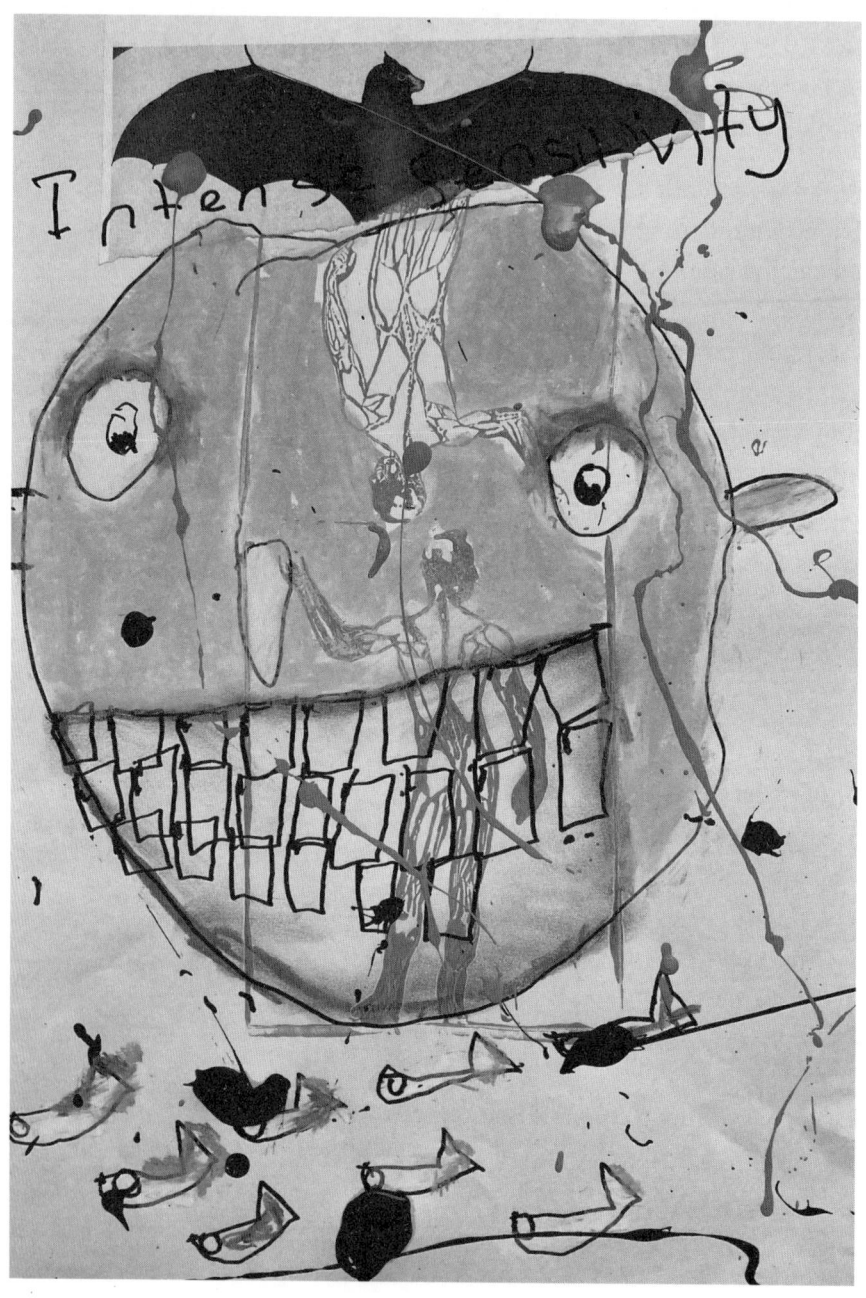

—

The above text was first written six years ago in the French Pyrenees as part of 'B is for Body', now revisited and reworked within the context of *a text that might engage with the risks of encounter, unsettling assumptions about the distinctions between host and guest; stranger and friend; self and other; documentarian and protagonist.*

Collages by Andrew & Eden Kötting, 2021–22

SINGLE TICKET
—
BRUNO DE WACHTER

TRANSLATED FROM THE DUTCH
BY PATRICK LENNON

On 1 August I travelled by train on a one-way ticket from my place of residence, Brussels, to Amsterdam. My friend Daniel received me well in his small but cosy flat in the Grachtengordel. In the early morning of 4 August, I left his place to walk back home on foot. I had to be back in Brussels by the end of the month.

Today is **Sunday 23 August**.

Rivierenhof, Antwerp, 11.30am. At a large block of flats with orange awnings under which people stripped to the waist are enjoying a late breakfast or early aperitif, I cross the Turnhoutsebaan – as quiet as if it were the middle of the night: even the tram is almost empty – and dive into the shade of the Rivierenhof. Walking has become an addiction. In the morning, when I'm well rested, I sense the wound-up spring of a little automaton in me, one of those toys that race along the floor when released. I don't walk blindly into walls, of course. I choose my path. It's usually easy, I know where I want to go, but sometimes, exceptionally, like now in the Rivierenhof, I hit a wall of doubt and get stuck.

My initial plan today was to walk in a more or less straight line to Mortsel, where I have booked a hotel for the coming night. Through the Rivierenhof, straight across Deurne-Zuid, past the airport and the Agfa-Gevaert factories to Oude God. A walk of at most three hours, leaving me plenty of time to look around. But now I don't like that idea. Lingering in memories no longer appeals to me; after all, I wanted to walk through the region of my birth at my normal walking pace, so why should I spend a whole afternoon in Mortsel doing nothing? Besides, the summery Sunday peace and quiet of the suburbs doesn't really attract me; I want action, I'm ready for the city! And then there's another reason for my hesitation, less easy to describe. For the first time, I feel that Brussels and the end of my journey are approaching, it won't take forever now. This makes me want to break through the deterministic nature of the journey from A to B, to ignore the destination and take side roads – the opposite of the final sprint.

In front of the Rivierenhof Castle, I get out the map of Antwerp and study the possibilities. I want to see the Scheldt. I could walk north from here to the Sportpaleis and from there due west towards the Scheldt. An appealing plan, but it feels unnatural to turn north while I have to go south. If I open the door to such departures, where will it end?

Hopping on two legs, I take the long park lane in a northwesterly direction. I'm heading north, says a voice inside me, and that's wrong; I should turn south again. But another voice shouts: Who cares! Tonight we shall be in Mortsel. It's Sunday, the sun is shining. The city! The Scheldt! The Noorderterras! Here I come!

At the Sportpaleis, my doubts have subsided. Delighted, I take the stinking tunnels under the motorway and railway and dive into the Stuivenberg neighbourhood – Onderwijsstraat, Erwtenstraat, Stuivenbergplein. I walk past what used to be the bathhouse to what used to be the north marshalling yard. The rusty train tracks have been removed to make way for a park.

In an exotic city, your attention is drawn to familiar elements, anchor points. In a well-known city, by contrast, your attention is automatically drawn to what is new. Park Spoor Noord only opened this summer, and together with many Antwerp citizens I walk along the gravel paths. It is all still a bit bare, the trees have yet to grow, but the pillars under the bridge have already been covered in spray paint.

> Graffiti is allowed on the pillars and walls under the bridge. Not on the ground, not on the water drains and not on other infrastructure in the park.
> Kind regards, The Park Coordination

Behind the bridge a shallow pool has been built in which children are busy splashing. The grass around it is filled with sunbathers. Shall I join them and lie down? I feel ashamed of my mountain boots and I don't dare expose my smelly socks in the open, among all those young mothers watching over their offspring. I continue my journey, over Italiëlei and Oude Leeuwenrui – familiar territory – until I reach the Scheldt.

Het Steen, Antwerp, 2.30pm. Sunbathing in the city, in full view of everyone, was not something she took for granted. A near-naked body among all those bricks, among all those dressed (up) people, it felt wrong. Even if you had on the most fashionable bikini, your body had not been made by a designer. On the beach, where everyone was radiant in their bare skin: well, that was something else. Or at a campsite, where all the city codes were thrown overboard anyway. At the swimming pool: naturally. But in the Stadspark, say, or at Park Spoor Noord, she didn't feel comfortable in a bikini.

She felt less embarrassment on the pontoon on the Scheldt. She would often walk or read at the water's edge to unwind, even in winter. Here, you were in the middle of the city and at the same time you were outside it: the river was empty and belonged to no one. Behind it stood the Linkeroever blocks, so motionless and dead that you could mistake them for rocks and mountains. Packed, clothed Antwerp was cut in half midway and was reflected in the empty, expansive water flowing back and forth indifferently on the other side of that line. Watching the Scheldt calmed her. Sometimes she tried to imagine what the view from the quay would have been like if the building mania of the sixties hadn't turned the marshes on the left bank into a high-rise district. Thanks to the rich reed growth and the tall poplars on the bank, this didn't require that much imagination.

She removed her jeans and T-shirt, carefully spread her towel on the warm wood and sat down. Sun cream.

Above the pontoon, the red flag with the Antwerp logo was flying, like a beach flag banning swimming. Further away, beyond the curve of the Scheldt, white clouds floated above the port's silos and cranes. Closing her eyes, she heard the city traffic far away. Closer by, there was the murmuring water, the drone of a ship's engine. She opened her eyes again: a blue ship called *Ramitha* was sailing inland. No one on deck. The waves rocked the pontoon gently. She lay on her back and sank into a half-sleep.

When she awoke, blinking against the bright sun, her skin felt as hot as a stove. The pontoon had risen noticeably with the tide.

Wolstraat, Antwerp, 3pm. 'A *bolleke*, please.' On the terrace of café Plansjee I manage to find a free seat among the tourists. The barman points at my rucksack:

'Exploring your own region?'

'That's right.'

'For real? No kidding?'

Soon I'm no longer sitting on the terrace but am inside, behind the bar, with a free beer in my hand.

The barman, Raf, vanishes outside to serve. He returns holding a collection of empty glasses, places them in the sink, puts on different music and turns back to me. A friend of his once took a holiday in his own city, he says. He told everyone he was going to Portugal, but in fact he was simply staying at a hotel in Antwerp. He went to different pubs and different shops than usual, walked up and down his own street now and then for fun. That whole week he didn't bump into a single person he knew. 'A crazy story. A crazy guy.'

Even before I've emptied my first glass, he draws a second. 'Another one on the house.' Raf is a construction worker, or so he says. He works two jobs at once for a few months and then heads off on a long trip. Africa. Asia. He's been doing this for years.

'I live off what I earn in the café, and I set aside my wages from the building industry. I just have to hang tight and then I'm off again. That's living, man. You've got to live! In a previous life I studied "Pol Soc". *Political and social sciences,*' he repeats emphatically, in a semi-official voice. 'That won't get you anywhere. But it's where you learn café life, and that's how you get work after all, as you can see.'

The free *bollekes* just keep on coming, and with each one Raf grows more personal, even though he himself hardly drinks. He was born in Lubumbashi, he says, and lived there until he was five. He doesn't have many concrete memories of his childhood any more, only fragments, atmospheres, a few anecdotes. But when he returned to the Congo for the first time three years ago, he was overwhelmed by 'a *mega* feeling of homecoming – those skies, those smells – wow! And if I can look after myself, it's because I got that from there too. *Article quinze*, you know: *débrouille-toi*.' Before that trip, he had never thought about how profoundly the Congo was embodied in him, but what a shock of recognition that was! Despite all the misery in that country, he felt so at ease there. 'You can't imagine', he says. But as I look at the nonchalant verve with which he dries the glasses, I can. 'Lubumbashi.'

'I wouldn't leave your rucksack there', Raf says by my fourth *bolleke*. 'Put it behind the bar.'

By the fifth, he asks me whether I want to help him serve.

'Not that I need help, but then you'd have something to do.'

He hands me a notepad and a biro, plus a list of four drinks that are sold out. I step outside, where the hot afternoon sun shines right in my face. Euphoric with surprise at the sudden change of roles, I take orders as if I've been working here for years.

'Sorry, madam, we're out of Fanta.'

'But it's on the drinks menu!'

'Ah, if it's on the drinks menu, that must explain why it's no longer in the fridge.'

'A Coke, then.'

'Coming up.'

By the sixth *bolleke*, Raf makes me a proposal: 'We should go on a journey together. One of those long treks in the Andes. What do you say? What's the best season to go there?'

But two sips later, he goes back on his words: 'Travelling with someone isn't a good idea. Twice I travelled with a girlfriend and twice it went utterly wrong. I'm not an easy person, I know that. And you don't look like you're run-of-the-mill either, by the way. So it just wouldn't work out. Don't get me wrong, you're a fine fellow, but travelling is something you should do alone. You're much more open to the world.'

I fully agree. 'We'll catch up afterwards,' I say. 'Here at the café.'

Meirbrug, Antwerp, 5pm. I walk out of the city along the route of tram 7, which I took so often as a child. Meirbrug, Oudaan, Nationale Bank, Harmonie, Sint-Willibrorduskerk. Dazed by the alcohol, my sense of time is on inactive and I fly along the footpaths – it's a good thing I'm carrying that heavy rucksack, or I really would break free from the ground and, swerving drunkenly this way and that, crash into the luxury flats on Fruithoflaan. I imagine that I am even going faster than the tram, because I walk without stops while the tram has to keep stopping, has to stop continually – *om de vijf botten*, every five bones, as we say – to let people off, doors open, doors closed – and hey, while walking along the Grote Steenweg I suddenly realise that this expression is nothing but an Antwerp version of the common Flemish expression *om de vijf voet*, every five feet, literally, although I've had trouble with that expression since childhood because *botten* made me think of bones and I didn't know how that computed with the meaning: is it about a man walking through a cemetery and who stops and bows his head *om de vijf botten*? Faster than the tram, then, which stops *om de vijf botten*, I walk along the Grote Steenweg, past a yellow sign with red letters that reads 'Mortsel', past the Sint-Theresiakerk with its green copper roof, past the De Castro bakery and the Agfa-Gevaert factories that tower above the residential areas, until I reach the-bridge-that-is-no-more, a place all Mortsel residents know by this name because this is where a railway bridge once crossed the road, before I was born. Sweating out the alcohol, I walk on, straight ahead, all the way to the tram terminus of Mortsel Oude God and Hotel Bristol, which I know so well from the outside, with its fake brown English-style awnings, but which I enter for the first time in my life. Behind the reception desk, there is a bronze Buddha and a plaster receptionist, but no one to help me. I wait patiently and try to look the man straight in the eye, but that is difficult because his glasses reflect the light. Finally, a live receptionist appears wearing the same suit, glasses and moustache as the imitation – I had expected something like this. The man puts my name down in the hotel register and hands me the key. He looks so serious that I don't dare make a joke.

Not only the reception, but the hotel as a whole appears to be a curiosity. With its carpets, imitation wooden doors and blue wall paint, the interior doesn't seem to have been renovated in years, but because it is all so clean and well maintained, it seems as if it is not the hotel interior of thirty years ago that has been smuggled into the present but that I myself am being sent back thirty years with a time machine. Only the yellowed ship photographs with the Agfa logo on the wall assure me that time has indeed gone by.

I take a cold shower and decide to go for a walk before dinner along the Cornelis de Herdtstraat in Hof van Rieth, where I grew up.

Cornelis De Herdtstraat, Mortsel, 8pm. It was her seventh birthday and the party was over. Throughout the summer holidays the street had been cordoned off as a play area, which is why her mum and dad had decided to hold the party not in the garden but at the front, in the driveway, so that all the children from the neighbourhood who happened to pass by could celebrate with them. They had built a small awning to provide shade during the hottest hours, and below it were a series of chairs that her dad had carried out from the kitchen and garage, and of course a table with sandwiches and sweets and drinks. Everything was decorated with brightly coloured garlands and balloons.

The last children had just left for home, but there was still a relaxed, exuberant atmosphere in the air, and while mum and dad were doing the washing up inside, she continued to blow bubbles on the pavement. She was just concentrating on a big bubble when she heard a man's voice nearby.

'Do you live here in this house?'

The bubble popped, the soap splattered in her face and she looked up: was he talking to her? A man in ruffled trousers was looking at her: 'So you live in this house?'

Silence.

'I used to live here, too.'

She quickly looked back to see if either her mum or dad was coming to assist her, before turning round to the man again. She couldn't get a word out of her throat.

'Yes, I lived here too, twenty-five, thirty years ago. When I was your age.'

She thought deeply but didn't know what to answer. Fortunately, he didn't insist and walked off down the street.

'Really?' her mother asked, when she told her about the man. 'It could be true, in the 1970s and 1980s a family with children lived here, I saw that in the land register.'

'What's a land register?'

It didn't leave her, the strange, unpleasant but also exciting thought that *other people had lived in this house before*, in *their* house. She herself had never lived anywhere else, so the man was talking about a time *when she didn't exist yet*. The thought hurt, the same kind of pain she felt when in the summer she had to go to bed while the grown-ups continued talking and drinking in the garden. She wanted to *be there*. She wanted to have been there, too, when that strange man had lived here in their house. She saw him sitting in the garden on a summer evening similar to this one – not as a child, but as the same adult man who had just addressed her.

'Did that man go to the toilet here too?'

'No doubt.'

'The same toilet as ours?'

'Probably.'

For the rest of the week, she saw ghosts of previous occupants: in the toilet, behind the bushes in the garden, in the cellar, even in her own attic room, which made it impossible for her to sleep at night.

'Did the first occupants come by horse and cart?'

'No, dear, our house isn't that old.'

'Then where did that cartwheel come from?'

'Good question! It was already here when we bought the house, and we left it. Don't you like it?'

From then on, the ghosts only appeared around the wheel in the garden, at dusk especially, and then she would sneak anxiously behind the bushes, as if to an altar, and have long conversations with earlier occupants. Sometimes she would smuggle in some food to make them happy. On bad days, when her mum and dad were cross, she would go there in the hope that her parents would make way for the previous residents. Leaning against the wall beside the wheel, sitting in the grass in front of the wheel or swaying on the branches of the rhododendron, she hoped at such times that the ghosts would take her to a distant and happy past, long before she was born.

Mechelsesteenweg, Mortsel, 10pm. Although the place is quite full, there's a quiet atmosphere in café De Voorspoed. The weekend is coming to an end and summer has had its time. No expectations are raised, people talk over a Trappist beer or a glass of wine. Pictures, anecdotes. A man yawns, asks for the bill. My own excited mood subsides along with the alcohol. I give my thoughts free rein over a cup of herbal tea, doodling little arrows on a beer mat.

The arrows remain meaningless for now. My thoughts are still veiled in a haze that is only slowly clearing.

I am seated at a table by the window, looking out at the traffic on the Mechelsesteenweg, at the Sint-Lutgardis school across the street with its limp flags for lack of wind, at an old man coming from the tram terminus who walks slowly by. I'm in Mortsel, where I lived for thirteen years and went to school for fifteen. Does it feel like a homecoming, as it did for Raf in the Congo? Do I feel that I belong here? Not really. I'm not easily overcome by homesickness, and in any case I've been away from here for so long. What I could feel is homesickness in time: nostalgia. During my rare, previous passages in the area, I did indeed become nostalgic, but today that feeling too is lacking: Mortsel leaves me indifferent. No, indifferent isn't the word, what I mainly feel today is estrangement. Or rather, astonishment. At what still looks the same after all this time and also at what has changed: new streets, time that has eaten away at houses, the cemetery that has become a park. Astonishment, too, at the fact that this place can function just as well as a stage in my walking tour as the strange Dutch villages I walked through in recent weeks.

Yes, all that, but the astonishment (slash estrangement) is mainly down to this: because the place that is most familiar to me of all places in the world is at the same time so far away from me. I have nothing to do with it anymore. Nowhere have I lived longer than here, and that during the influential years of my childhood, but today the familiar Mortsel seems foreign to me; not the place itself, but *its familiar character* is foreign to me, like something left over from an earlier time, while it has long since lost its function. Like my navel, I think, and I put down my pen, run my hand over my stomach and feel the scar through my T-shirt: a super-familiar place, but when I think about it, about the former function of that place, I'm suddenly flung out of my familiar body, because have I – *me*, damn it, with this body here – ever been a newborn? In a previous life, perhaps!

I nibble the speculoos biscuit served with the tea and take my notebook out of my jacket. On a white page I write 'homesickness' dash 'nostalgia'.

Chapter 1: People and their environment. People are never one with their environment. There is an environment that is constantly changing. And there are people who are also constantly changing, under the influence of, among other things, the changing environment. To be able to stick it out as a changing person in a changing environment without getting seasick, we create stories: I, here, now. In their immutable nature, these stories can never do full justice to the changing self in the changing environment, they are always behind the facts, as a result of which a black hole continues to exist between reality and how we see that reality.

I turn over the sheet and write:

Chapter 2: Homesickness. If you suddenly find yourself in an environment that is very different and you are not used to such changeability, you won't be able to complete your story, which will give you a shock; in a state of panic, you will want to return as quickly as possible to a place where your story does seem to fit. People suffer from homesickness because they have lived for a long time in the illusion of a stable environment, of a place that changes so slowly that the story can adjust itself to the changes.

On a new page:

People who move around a lot, by contrast, get used to constantly rewriting the story and know that there will always be a black hole between story and reality: they feel at home everywhere and nowhere, and don't find that problematic. In order to fill this black hole, every place comes with a longing for another, ideal place, and even though they do not necessarily cherish the illusion of reaching that ideal, it keeps them going. However, when that movement comes to a halt due to circumstances, for example during a visit to a place from the past, they feel ...

On another new page:

Chapter 3: Nostalgia. Once more it is about a discrepancy between story and environment, but this time the cause is not in the environment, but in themselves. While they were constantly occupied with the changing environment, the change in their own selves passed them by. Faced with their new selves, they don't know what to do with it, especially not in the old environment that they happen to find themselves in again, and in a state of panic they long for their former selves, for the longing of the past. Nostalgia is a longing for a longing of the past, born of the illusion of the unchanging self.

I read that last sentence three more times and suddenly I feel terribly tired – is it because of the walk, the alcohol, or all the abstract ideas I'm pursuing so stubbornly and trying to capture in words? Still, with one last little bit of concentration, I write an afterthought:

Because it is not reality that we long for in nostalgia but the stories and desires that were projected onto reality, we can also be nostalgic for a time that we ourselves never experienced. A few fragments of image or text handed down can be enough to set our storytelling machine in motion. Such nostalgia, too, rests on the illusion that we can simply move ourselves through time and still remain ourselves; in other words, it denies that without the here and now we ourselves would not be as we are, we would be someone else, with yet other desires, for yet another environment and yet another time.

Drowsy, I close the door of the café behind me and walk into the street. I let a car go by and cross the road in the direction of the hotel, although the pedestrian light is red. When I reach the central reservation, the light changes to green.

THE RED DREAM
—
ADAM CHRISTENSEN

The coke made me alert. The ketamine made me crack jokes. I had another martini. Grace pointed out I was in the leaning chair in a crunching foetal position. The jokes had faded. I had gone silent. I climbed into Husky Thirst's new built mezzanine 6 feet above the floor from where I had hallucinated Grace's silicone tits arguing with Jizzer's cornrow extensions. Faint conversations below. Red dots forming in the ceiling. The dots descended. The room turned red. I hovered out of the duvet leaving it behind naked. Flew silently behind a shadow. The red slowly faded. I found myself by the entrance to the toilet. My feet firmly on the cold concrete floor. A leather sling hovering next to me. I was confused by this sudden emerging of reality. The guilt. Husky Thirst was wondering why I had followed him to the toilet. I was too. I told him I needed a piss. No piss came out. I went back to bed. Slowly the red dots descended on me once more.

    My phone vibrated across the wooden boards of the mezzanine. My mother video-calling. Lise on her way out. Lise, my second mother of 34 years. Last chance to say goodbye. I felt it the last time she video-called. Lise ill as fuck sitting on the toilet having a shit, smoking. Giving me compliments which was very unusual. Her face was way too close to the tablet. Warped by the wide-angle built-in camera. It felt like a declaration. A dying one. She whispered.

Det er lidt chokerende
Den måde du synger på
Nu har jeg sagt det
Jeg forstår det bare ikke helt
Den gang du sang til forårskoncerten
I don't want to miss a thing med Aerosmith
Wow
Hold nu kæft
Det var vildt
Du ved jeg elsker dig

Det der du gør
Det er vildt
Hold kæft
Vildt
Jeg bliver bare lidt chokeret
Altså den måde du synger på nu
Du skal ikke lytte til mig
Det er vildt
Du er vild
Bliv ved
Bliv ved med at lave det der skørre noget
Du skal bare være vild
Vær vild
Jeg elsker dig
Adam
Jeg elsker dig
Og du skal bare være vild
Jeg elsker dig
Vær vild
Du skal bare gøre det der, du gør
Stop ikke med at være dig
Jeg elsker dig
Du ved jeg elsker dig

I packed a suitcase. Badly. I found it hard travelling. My first time leaving my compound since the lockdown had started. No tests were needed. The Danish minx hadn't contracted a possibly dangerous variant of the virus yet. No mass graves filled with the little buggers sanctioned by the discombobulated government.

When I arrived in my childhood home in Vejen, Lise was lying in a hospital bed in the living room. The dining table was gone. Given to the charity shop along with the glass cabinet, shelves, leaning chair. Lise's duvet was covered with my teenage bed sheets. A large print of Madonna's face. Leather fingerless gloves. Bracelets. Who's That Girl/True Blue period. Lise couldn't speak. Her eyes didn't focus properly. I could tell she was trying. She knew I was there. Wasn't able to crack a sharp remark. No words. No movement. Her body had let go. Her mind holding on, viciously. On the third night my mum and I had stayed awake. My sister drove over in the early hours. The nurse dropped by shortly after. Lise's breathing had a rhythm. Slime stuck in her throat vibrating, making a repetitive beat. The nurse gave Lise a shot of morphine. I held Lise's hand continuously.

> Lise stopped breathing.
> Her eyes rolled into position.
> Her pupils moving.
> She looked right at me.
> I let out a strange sound.
> My mum and my sister jumped out of the sofa
> Lise squeezed my hand hard
> She lifted her other hand for my sister and mum to grab
> Her eyelids slowly slid over her eyes
> The low-hanging lips drew into a cheeky smile
> It was a cute smile
> A naughty smile
> She went silent
> We were silent
> We cried
> Held each other close for as long as we each needed
> The nurse cried too
> She was given hugs as well

Not long after, the home care came round. I helped them wash Lise's naked body. Combed her entangled silky grey hair. Gently. My mum went upstairs. Came down with a specially selected suit. My mum cried tears of happiness seeing Lise all beautifully dressed. She picked flowers from the garden. Placed them in Lise's folded hands. Emily did practical research online. Ordering the undertakers, an urn. The neighbours came over with flowers from their gardens. Laid them next to Lise. She smelled fresh. I kissed her cold cheek. In the morning I went to the shops. Arranged a buffet in the garden. Light gusts of wind shaking the large bamboos. Warmest day of the year. Christina came over. Anders couldn't make it. Work. Lise had started to swell slightly. Purple marks on her neck. The undertakers needed help carrying her out into the coffin in the front garden. I wrote a message on the wooden lid. We sang a little song as she was driven away.

    I went for a walk along Kongeåen. The river that once divided Denmark from Slesvig and Holsten. The sun bouncing off the fast moving stream. A flock of cows pushing me against the fence. Allowing me to stroke the rough fur between their eyes. Licking my newly painted nails. Realising I had no apples. Running off. Over the hill. Through the woods. The new moon rising from the bendy stream. Walking the long way back. Stopping for a drink at the local bodega. Only place open.

    Hailing rain on tin ceiling. Mum walking around restless. Trying to pack her bag. Holding Lise's ashes close to her body. I calmed her down. Laid her on the sofa. I was next to her on a rolled-out mattress. I woke again. Mum was not on the sofa. Not in the bed. I sat on the sofa about to call my sister in Kolonihavehuset on the next allotment. My eyes adjusted to a silhouette sitting in the chair by the window. My mum sleeping upright clinging on to Lise's ashes. Her packed suitcase parked next to her. She said when it rained in Malaysia they would always have a packed suitcase ready in case of floods. Evacuating.

We sailed out in a wooden boat in Vejle Fjord. The sun had come out. Calm waves. Flock of birds flying over the mast. Emily's boyfriend was holding on to my mum's belt while she spread Lise's ashes over the stern. The sailor brought me a beer. A shot of Gammel Dansk. Warm coffee from a flask. I sang a cover of the song Madonna wrote for her mother. Wind picking up. Swallowing my words. Deafening the whining accordion notes.

Everything was red
I climbed off a hard rock
Runes carved into it
Ancient messages
Walked through a dungeon
Burning torches
Flames all red
An open cave
Slaughtered animal half devoured hanging over wood turned to coal
A hairy man
Muscular
Snoring
Asleep on top of a fur still dripping blood
Red
I backed up
Quietly
Crept out the gate
Half-dressed
Walked down ancient streets
Red
Reached a lake
A castle on top of a hill
Koldinghus
Local landmark

>The castle Spanish soldiers accidentally burned to the ground by stacking too many logs in the fireplace
>I suddenly remembered I had been drinking vodka martinis with Anders and Christina earlier that evening
>Anders's new flat
>Grilling steak
>Homemade chips
>He had gone to sleep in the living room
>Lending me his bed
>I sat down on a bench underneath the castle by the lake
>Dreaded having to trace my steps back to his
>Having to wake him in order to get back in
>Explaining how I left without a jacket
>Keys
>Only one sock
>'Its all a blur ... man ... must have been the vodka martinis'

An Indian boy walked past with a joint hanging from his big lips. Exchange student at the design school. He sat down next to me. Passed me the joint. I took a puff. Kissed him. Got stuck. His tongue climbed down my throat. Swallowed my moan. Red turned to pink. He lifted me up. He was so tall. So skinny. So strong. Carried me to his student apartment. City square. Dropped me halfway out the window. Slid my Calvin Klein g-string over my left arse cheek. Pressed his expanding fat cock inside me. Pushed his fingers down my throat. Deafening the cries. Screams. Moans. He asked me if he was hurting me. I said no. Why? He said cos I had tears coming down my face. Happy tears I told him. We smoked another joint on his bed. Fucked once more. Before I walked back to the dungeon.

THE MYSTERY OF LANGUAGE

—

XIAOLU GUO

One spring afternoon, I walked into a 'Blume für immer' in East Berlin. My eyes were caught by bouquets of fresh pink tulips. The seller, an Asian woman, asked with a smile: 'Welche Blumen möchtest du?'

She had a strong accent. And I could vaguely make out that she asked what flowers I was looking for. I answered with my primitive hybrid German: 'Danke. Wie viel für your tulips?'

She stared at me, her eyes shining. And within seconds, she answered in Mandarin Chinese: 'Qi Yuan.'

That meant: *7 euros.* I smiled to her, nodding, and brought out my wallet.

But that was not the end of the conversation. She wrapped the flowers with paper and continued to gaze intently at me. Without even asking if I was from Zhejiang province in China, she launched into a question in my hometown dialect.

'Ni dao yi da xi a? Ju da er?'

That meant: *Are you here sightseeing, or do you live here?* Her Zhejiang dialect was absolutely authentic. I could even tell that she had a local accent from my little town – Taizhou, a place by the coast in my province.

I answered with my Taizhou dialect: 'Lei lu you,' meaning I was here for tourism, even though I was in Berlin for different reasons.

She handed me the bouquet of tulips. We briefly looked at each other, our smiles revealing something I could not quite articulate in words. I didn't ask how she made out that we were from the same little town in China, despite my only speaking a broken German sentence.

Goethe famously said: 'He who knows no foreign languages knows nothing of his own.' Since both the flower seller and I spoke a foreign language – German – to begin with, I wonder if this was proof that she and I had a sixth sense about language.

We are born into language. Language is already there before we form our body, our identity and our path of life. Right now, I am writing in English in a blue armchair in London. But on exactly the same chair at exactly the same time, I speak Chinese to my child. This seems to be beyond my control. And if I'm conversing with my dead parents in my writing, or in my dreams, our speech is in Taizhou dialect, a language the Berlin flower seller speaks. How we live through languages is a mystery. A language is like the shadow our own body casts in the sun. It moves along with us, even when we are running somewhere else. It clings to us, whether we migrate across oceans or never leave the village we were born in.

EPILOGUE:
COMME UNE LETTRE
—
MIREILLE GANSEL

Dear friends, Thérèse and Juliette,

Arriving at the end of this book, turning the last page, the words you asked me to write come to me as a letter: I would say a last letter, or a postscript to all and each of those twenty texts which resonate for me as letters written with the ink of life, with such truthful words, each one listening to, listening in, each page like a mirror on deepest waters.

Letters: as a quintessence, one of the secret red threads running all the way along from *the very first letters of my alphabet* to those written, received or sent, or just traces of memories, of storytelling, of something whispered to oneself, half in a dream, half in greatest solitude, *childish letters, melancholy letters, voyages in time* or just letters about *the dangers of going to the post office in Kathmandu... the first letter you sent me... my last letter to you...*

With all the space and freedom given by letter-writing, a voyage *across language and generations, movements of words*, discovering a *sixth sense about language*, exploring our *mother tongue, a foreign language* – yes, the letter as the first and ultimate sign/signature of a soul, of a life, as traces on the pavement from the homeless, black traces on the pages of Mohammad – *I draw draw draw Mohammad* – or pained by Eden whose *SYNTAX is a tree-like structure, spreading out from a combination of limited root words and ideas...*

Mysteriously woven among those letters, written without a recipient, whispered somewhere in the park of someone's childhood, *something happened in this park, which left a big black hole in my memory. I am here to uncover what this event was.* These poignant lines will haunt us like some unresolved enigma until, suddenly, like a consolation, a response, towards the end, opening a space of remembrance, of dream: *In order to fill this black hole, every place comes with a longing for another, ideal place.*

glimpse – detour – wayward: a constellation of words traces a crystallography of meanings, nuances, depths, which irradiate through this pile of letters: the encounter enlightens.

The encounter: **Ich und Du**: **I and you**: *I in itself does not exist, but only the basic word* **I–you**, **I–it** *– the basic word* **I–you** *creates the relationship* (Martin Buber) – and here, in these pages:
> all the words to express **you**; *the other outsider foreigner stranger* and only this one word to express the relation: **within**

A key for me to enter into the meaning and topography of this word **within**, in this very precise context, has been Yirmiyyahu Yovel's book *The Other Within: The Marranos – Split Identity and Emerging Modernity*:
> The conversos, a mixed or divided self, in which the Other is preserved within the Self and partly constitutes it... The Marrano story breaks integral identities and transcends any single culture.

***

Each of these texts, traced, written with the ink of empathy – yes, a whole lexicon, or, better, like a long poem with only those words of 'the humanity in the human being':
> *benevolent travelling source*
> *helped me to become a more compassionate person*
> *empathy translated into the streets*
> *I love the fact that people are different. If there's anything to be achieved, it's to celebrate that difference and not judge it.*

> *I don't actually hope to achieve anything other than some*
> *human moments*
> *The emotional heart of something*
> *they reveal... their humanity*
> *Generous and kind*
> *kin matters*
> *solidarity of purpose and perception*
> *a different kind of trust and a different kind of feeling of*
> *being listened to*

Maybe the magic of this anthology – so rare, unique – is its distinctly human aura:

> *my work is really about healing*
> *the tenderness with which they are revealed bridges and*
> *briefly defeats the gulf of otherness*

Maybe its secret soul is the deep feeling of being welcomed: I as reader, no longer an outsider. I am invited to enter, and to share:

> *I give hospitality to the other that I will become for him, and to*
> *the other him that he will become partly for me*
> *I accept the deal because your love for me is there, untouched*

Maybe, too, it's the deep vocation of your art:

> *the film gives us hospitality*

Maybe I would say the same words, for the work of 'translation': translating as I experience and conceive it: on the terrain.

Turning to the encounter of poets in exile, banned in their own country, poets in places and lives ruined by bombs, I feel such a deep resonance:

Making films and travelling means to move around in unsafe zones, to be always ready for surprises... Every detour changes the destination.
Ruth Beckermann

My work is really about choosing to see the light in a person... we choose what we see... we look inward first.
Khalik Allah

To make space inside oneself for what one does not know and may never know.
Andrea Luka Zimmerman

We are made up of fragments of others...
The level of personal engagement required when trying to convey the being of another person, especially someone very different from oneself... an act of self-dislocation... part of the attraction and part of the risk
David MacDougall

In gratitude to you all for the good that each of your pages does to me.

CONTRIBUTOR BIOGRAPHIES

Khalik Allah is a New York-based photographer and filmmaker. Khalik's passion for photography was sparked when he began photographing members of the Wu-Tang Clan with a camera he borrowed from his dad. The people he photographs on the corner of 125th Street and Lexington Avenue in Harlem have been his central inspiration, which also extends to documentary film with *Field Niggas* (2015), a chronicle of summer nights spent on that corner. Khalik shoots with a manual, analogue film camera, as photography and filmmaking form a Venn diagram in his work. His other films include the documentaries *Black Mother* (2018) and *IWOW: I Walk on Water* (2020).

Ruth Beckermann was born in Vienna, where she also spent her childhood. In 1978 she co-founded the distribution company filmladen, in which she was active for seven years. It was during this period that Beckermann started to make films and write books, and since 1985 she has worked as a writer and filmmaker. Her films include *The Paper Bridge* (1987) and *East of War* (1996). Her film *The Dreamed Ones* (2016) was selected at many international festivals and won several awards. *The Waldheim Waltz* premiered at the Berlinale in 2018, where it won the award for Best Documentary Film. In 2019 Beckermann conceived the multimedia installation *Joyful Joyce* for the Salzburg Festival. Her film *MUTZENBACHER* premiered as part of Encounters at the Berlinale 2022 and won the award for Best Film.

Jon Bang Carlsen is a film director. He graduated from the Danish Film School in 1976 and has written and directed more than thirty films, both documentary and feature. Carlsen's signature hybrid style combines documentary and fictional interpretations, and many of his documentaries are visually and symbolically powerful, often staged portraits of marginal figures and milieus. From 1977 onwards, *mise-en-scène* with real characters began to play a very important part in his productions, and this method is detailed in his meta-film *How to Invent Reality* (1996). Carlsen says: 'To me, documentaries are no more "real" than fiction films, and fiction films are no more fabulating than documentaries. There is no "reality" that cannot be seen from a different angle and be revealed as a dream. To describe the world, you have to define the truth in a way that does not exclude lies.'

Adam Christensen is a London-based artist whose working practice is primarily realised through textiles, music and installation. His research reflects upon the mise-en-scène of a subject, its construction and representation, blurring the boundaries between everyday life and fiction. Based on his immediate experiences, coloured by the theatricality of the everyday, the spectacle of domesticity, chance encounters and emotional and physical dramas, Christensen conveys these experiences through his performances. Recent exhibitions include *You Might Wanna Stay Over*, Rønnesbækholm, Næstved (2022); *I'm not done with you yet*, Goldsmiths CCA, London (2019); *Criminal Longing 3*, Almanac Projects, London (2019); *Shitty Heartbreaker*, Overgaden, Copenhagen (2018); and *Staging Realities 1*, Kunstverein, Hamburg (2018). He also performs with the music project Ectopia, which was Wysing Arts Centre's band-in-residence in 2016.

From his base in Brussels, **Bruno De Wachter** splits his time between work as a technical copywriter and his own walking and writing projects. He has published essays and prose in various magazines, including the Flemish literature magazine *nY* and *Les Carnets du Paysage* (France). He has started working on prose inspired by long-distance walking. He has a special interest in the tension between the global and the local, and in the interrelations between the human body, language and landscape. He sometimes organises group walks and participates in artistic projects that are related to literature and/or walking.

Annie Ernaux grew up in Normandy, studied at Rouen University and later taught at secondary schools. From 1977 to 2000 she was a professor at the Centre National d'Enseignement par Correspondance. Her books, in particular *A Man's Place* (1983) and *A Woman's Story* (1987), have become contemporary classics in France. *The Years* won the Prix Renaudot in France in 2008, the Premio Strega in Italy in 2016, and was shortlisted for the Man Booker International Prize in 2019. In 2017, Ernaux was awarded the Marguerite Yourcenar Prize for her life's work.

Gareth Evans is a London-based writer, editor, film and event producer and Adjunct Moving Image Curator at the Whitechapel Gallery. He hosts the LRB Screen at Home programme and curates for Forum of the Future Porto, Estuary, First Light, Flipside and Swedenborg film festivals. He has conceived and curated numerous film and event seasons across the UK, including 'John Berger: Here Is Where We Meet', 'All Power to the Imagination! 1968 & its Legacies', and major retrospectives of the films of Jem Cohen, Mike Dibb, Alexander Kluge, Chris Marker, Jonathan Meades, Xiaolu Guo and Laura Mulvey and Peter Wollen. He edited the international moving image magazine *Vertigo* and now co-edits for House Sparrow Press, publishing original titles by John Berger and Anne Michaels, among others.

Jane Fawcett was born in Wensleydale, North Yorkshire and spent most of her youth there. She is an artist and a writer. She has exhibited, presented and published in a wide range of contexts, including at Coleman Project Space, Camden Arts Centre, PEER and the ICA in London; Triangle, Marseille; Legion Projects; TENT, Rotterdam; Kölnischer Kunstverein, Cologne; and HEAD, Geneva. She edits the magazine *Friends Jobs*, which asks contributors to consider their 'jobs' and to excavate these roles through fantasy.

Mireille Gansel has published translations of a number of distinguished poets including Nelly Sachs, Peter Huchel, and the great contemporary poet Reiner Kunze, whose work she introduced to French readers, as well as letters by Paul Celan to Nelly Sachs. After living in Hanoi in the seventies, she published the first volume of classical Vietnamese poetry translated into French. For a long time she contributed to *La Quinzaine Littéraire*, the literary magazine founded by Maurice Nadeau. *Une petite fenêtre d'or* and the poetry collection *Comme une lettre* were published in France in 2017 followed by *Maison d'âmes* (a volume of memoirs) in 2018, all with Éditions La Coopérative. She is also the author of *Larmes de neige* (2006) and *Chronique de la rue Saint-Paul* (2010). Her lyrical memoir, *Translation as Transhumance* – translated into English by Ros Schwartz – was published in 2014 and has contributed significantly to the field of translation studies. In 2018, Mireille became the Laureate of the Great Prize of Translation Etienne Dolet-Sorbonne Université. Other awards include the Khoury-Ghata poetry prize, the Gérald de Nerval translation prize, an English PEN Award, and a French Voices Award.

Xiaolu Guo is a Chinese-British novelist, filmmaker and memoirist. Her novels include *A Concise Chinese-English Dictionary for Lovers* (2007) and *I Am China* (2014). Her memoir *Once Upon a Time in the East* (2017) won the National Book Critics Circle Award 2017 and was shortlisted for the RSL Ondaatje Award, Costa Book Awards and Folio Prize. Her most recent novel is *A Lover's Discourse*, shortlisted for the Goldsmiths Prize 2020 and longlisted for the Orwell Prize. Guo has also directed a dozen films, including *How Is Your Fish Today*, selected at Sundance 2017; and *UFO in Her Eyes*, which premiered at Toronto International Film Festival 2011. Her feature film *She, a Chinese* received the Golden Leopard at the Locarno Film Festival 2009. Her documentary *We Went to Wonderland* (2008) was shown at MoMA, New York, and she has had retrospectives at the Whitechapel Gallery, London (2019), Greek Film Archive, Athens (2018) and Cinémathèque Suisse, Lausanne (2011). She was a visiting professor at Columbia University and Baruch College, New York. She lives in London.

Umama Hamido, born in Lebanon and currently based in London, is an artist and filmmaker. Her work focuses on lived and shared experiences of immigration, as she questions our relation to traumatic spaces and how the formation of the self is affected by separation from homeland and the exile's gaze. Hamido has a BA in Theatre from the Lebanese University and an MA in Performance from Goldsmiths, University of London. She has performed at various galleries across the UK, including Turner Contemporary, Margate; Modern Art Oxford; Toynbee Studios, London; Mosaic Rooms, London; and New Art Exchange, Nottingham; and at festivals including Otherfiel, SPILL Festival, Dublin Live Art Festival, Les Rencontres à l'Échelle, and Arab Women Artists Now Festival. She also performs in the collaborative projects of others and teaches and translates Arabic.

Therese Henningsen is a filmmaker and programmer based in London. Her filmmaking often takes shape through the encounter with the person(s) filmed and the direction this takes. She is currently working on a practice-led PhD in Media Arts at Royal Holloway, University of London that is closely linked to *Strangers Within* and the idea of 'documentary as encounter'. Her films *Slow Delay* (2018) and *Maintenancer* (with Sidsel Meineche Hansen, 2018) have been shown and exhibited at Whitechapel Gallery, London; Chisenhale Gallery, London; Venice Biennale; Close-Up Film Centre, London; Whitstable Biennale; SMK – Statens Museum for Kunst, Copenhagen; Cryptofiction; and Liberated Film Club, among others. She is a member of the film collectives Sharna Pax and Terrassen, both engaging with the social life of film. Therese came to filmmaking through anthropology and holds an MA in Visual Anthropology from Goldsmiths, University of London. She teaches on the MA Ethnographic and Documentary Film and MA Docfiction at UCL.

Since his first film, *Lift*, in 2001, **Marc Isaacs** has made more than sixteen creative documentaries for the likes of the BBC, Channel 4 and cinema. His films have won Grierson, Royal Television Society and BAFTA awards as well as international film festival prizes. In 2006 Marc had a retrospective at the prestigious Lussas documentary film festival in France, and his work has been included in numerous documentary books and academic studies. In 2008 he received an honorary doctorate from the University of East London for his documentary work. Marc has been a guest tutor at numerous universities and film schools in the UK and overseas, including the London Film School and the National Film and Television School. He is currently an Associate Professor at University College London. A complete box set of his films, entitled *From 'Lift' to 'The Road'*, was released by Second Run DVD in 2018, and a full retrospective of his work was shown at the Centre Pompidou, Paris, in 2022. His latest film, *The Filmmaker's House* (2021), is screening at festivals worldwide.

Mary Jiménez Freeman-Morris was born in Peru. She first studied architecture in Lima before pursuing studies in cinema at INSAS film school in Belgium. A writer and director for more than thirty years, she has also taught cinema in Belgium, Cuba and Switzerland. She actively collaborates with SoundImageCulture (SIC) in Brussels. Mary's films include *Du verbe aimer* (1984), *La Position du lion couché* (2006), *Le Dictionnaire selon Marcus* (2009) and *Héros sans visages* (2012), all of which have been selected at numerous festivals around the world.

Juliette Joffé is an award-winning filmmaker and lecturer based in Belgium. Her films have been shown at festivals such as Visions Du Réel; FIDMarseille; Open City Documentary Film Festival, Whitechapel Gallery; Asolo Art Film Festival; and Sheffield Fringe, among others. Her first film, *Maybe Darkness* (*Peut-être le noir*), won the Wildcard for Best Documentary awarded by the Flemish Film Board (VAF). Her second film, *The Hero with a Thousand Faces* (*Le Héros aux mille visages*), won Best Short Film at Mostra Internazionale del Cinema di Genova. In her most recent film, *Next year, we will leave* (2021), she is interested in questioning the documentary form as a type of encounter in which the border between self and other, stranger and friend, director and character, are blurred. She currently teaches the course 'Documentary as Encounter' at Open City Docs School, London, with Therese Henningsen and runs the documentary course at Brussels-based art school Preparts.

Andrew Kötting was born in Elmstead Woods in 1959. After some early forays into market trading and scrap-metal dealing he graduated with a master's degree from The Slade, London, in 1989. **Eden Kötting** was born in Guy's Hospital in 1988 with a rare neurological disorder, Joubert syndrome. She grew up in London and developed a keen interest in drawing and painting. Together they have made work for over twenty years, including their film *Gallivant* (1996), a road/home movie about their four-month trip around the coast of Britain along with Andrew's grandmother and Eden's great-grandmother Gladys. Andrew and Eden have worked on numerous multimedia art projects, which include exhibitions, installations, performances, LPs, CDs and bookworks. In 2015 they also began their collaboration with the animator Glenn Whiting and went on to create short films for Channel 4, Random Acts, HOME and the BFI. Their most recent work, *Diseased & Disorderly*, was made during Covid-19 lockdown and dealt with the themes of family as safe havens, sanctuary and the power of collaboration. They share a studio in St Leonards-on-Sea, where they are developing a VR project, *The Tell-Tale Rooms*. Andrew and Eden had their first major London show at New Art Projects in June 2022 and are also part of the collective Project Art Works, who were shortlisted for the Turner Prize in 2021.

David MacDougall is a maker of documentary and ethnographic films and a writer on cinema. He has filmed in East Africa, Australia, Sardinia and India. With his wife Judith MacDougall he produced the 'Turkana Conversations' trilogy in Kenya in 1973–74, including the film *The Wedding Camels* (1977) and later *Photo Wallahs* (1991), about Indian photography, as well as eight films about Australian Aboriginal communities, including *Takeover* (1980) and *Sunny and the Dark Horse* (1986). Among his other films are *To Live with Herds* (1972), *Tempus de Baristas* (1993), *SchoolScapes* (2007) and *Under the Palace Wall* (2014). In 1997–2000 he conducted a study of the Doon School in northern India, producing *Doon School Chronicles* (2000) and four other films, followed by films about the Rishi Valley School in South India and *Gandhi's Children* (2008), about a shelter for homeless children in New Delhi. He is the author of numerous journal articles and four books: *Transcultural Cinema* (1998), *The Corporeal Image* (2006), *The Looking Machine* (2019) and *The Art of the Observer* (2022). He is presently Honorary Professor at the Research School of Humanities and the Arts, Australian National University, Canberra. In his most recent project, Childhood and Modernity, he helped groups of Indian children conduct research and make films in their own communities.

Filmmaker, writer, composer **Trinh T. Minh-ha** is a Distinguished Professor of the Graduate School at the University of California, Berkeley. Her work includes: nine feature-length films, including *What About China?* (2021), *Forgetting Vietnam* (2016), *Night Passage* (2004), *The Fourth Dimension* (2001), *A Tale of Love* (1996), *Shoot for the Contents* (1991), *Surname Viet Given Name Nam* (1989), *Naked Spaces* (1985) and *Reassemblage* (1982), honoured in over sixty-four retrospectives around the world; several large-scale multimedia installations, including *In Transit* (Manifesta 13, Marseille, 2020), *L'Autre marche* (Musée du Quai Branly, Paris, 2006–9), *Old Land New Waters* (3rd Guangzhou Triennial, China, 2008; Okinawa Museum of Fine Arts, 2007), *The Desert is Watching* (Kyoto Biennial, 2003); and numerous books, such as *Lovecidal: Walking with The Disappeared* (2016), *D-Passage: The Digital Way* (2013), *Elsewhere, Within Here* (2011), *Cinema Interval* (1999) and *Woman, Native, Other: Writing Postcoloniality and Feminism* (1989). Her many awards include the Prix Bartók at the Jean Rouch Festival in Paris; the 2022 New:Vision Award at CPH:DOX Film Festival in Copenhagen; the 2022 Golden Gate Persistence of Vision Award at the San Francisco International Film Festival; the 2014 Wild Dreamer Lifetime Achievement Award at the Subversive Film Festival, Zagreb; the 2012 Lifetime Achievement Award from Women's Caucus for Art; the 2012 Critics' Choice Book Award of the American Educational Studies Association; the 2006 Trailblazers Award at MIPDoc in Cannes, France; and the 1991 American Film Institute National Independent Filmmaker Maya Deren Award.

Toni Morrison (1931–2019) was an acclaimed American author, editor and professor. She was the author of many novels, including *The Bluest Eye* (1970), *Song of Solomon* (1977) and *Beloved* (1987), for which she was awarded the Pulitzer Prize for Fiction. She won the Nobel Prize in Literature in 1993.

Andrea Luka Zimmerman is a filmmaker and artist whose engaged practice calls for a profound reimagining of the relationship between people, place and ecology. Focusing on marginalised individuals, communities and experience, her practice employs imaginative hybridity and narrative reframing, alongside reverie and a creative waywardness. Informed by suppressed histories, and alert to sources of radical hope, the work prioritises an enduring and equitable coexistence. Andrea's feature-length films have won numerous awards internationally. Andrea is Professor of Possible Film at Central Saint Martins. www.fugitiveimages.org.uk.

FILMOGRAPHY

This filmography was the starting point of the discussion that led to *Strangers Within*. It was initially conceived solely as a film programme for the Whitechapel Gallery and grew into a wider research project comprising this anthology.

IWOW: I Walk on Water, dir. Khalik Allah (2020; 200 min)
Returning to the intersection of 125th Street and Lexington Avenue in East Harlem, Khalik Allah centres this film on his long-time friendship with Frenchie, a homeless Haitian man, while also documenting his recent life: his relationships with his former girlfriend and an inner circle of friends, including Fab 5 Freddy, members of the Wu-Tang Clan and his mother.

Those Who Go Those Who Stay, dir. Ruth Beckermann (2013; 75 min)
Rain on a window pane, a fire engine, a tomcat with innumerable offspring: it is an intentionally unintentional gaze that allows for chance encounters, for stories and memories – leads that Ruth Beckermann follows across Europe and the Mediterranean. Nigerian asylum seekers in Sicily, an Arab musician in Galilee, nationalists drunk on beer in Vienna, the Capitoline Wolf, and three veiled young women trying for minutes to cross a busy road in Alexandria. Threads, cloth and textiles pop up like bookmarks in a fabric of movement, of travelling or seeking refuge. *Those Who Go Those Who Stay* is a story of being on the move, both in the world and in one's own life.

Addicted to Solitude, dir. Jon Bang Carlsen (1999; 60 min)
After the fall of apartheid, a Danish film director arrives in South Africa. Instead of making the film he intended, he finds himself submerged in solitude, listening to the reflections of two white South African women of different backgrounds. 'I travelled to South Africa to find a white family on a desolate farm and film how they faced the new days of equality after Apartheid, but I soon lost my way both on the endless roads and in my mind. Instead the film became a story about two different white women who both experienced tragic losses in the midst of a white community that wasn't too fond of the future.'

Far and Near, dir. Xiaolu Guo (2003; 22 min)
Leaving her country for the first time, a young Chinese writer wanders on a wild mountain in Wales. Through the beautiful and empty landscape, and the people she meets, she enters a dreamlike world where memories of life in rapidly developing Beijing, and a childhood in a poor fishing village, return to her. She contemplates loneliness and is unexpectedly haunted by stories of tragic deaths.

On Akka's Shore, dir. Umama Hamido (2018; 60 min)
On Akka's Shore is a fictional memoir of Umama Hamido and her friend Tareq Al Jazzar, based on hallucinations, dreams and out-of-body experiences. Scenes slip between Akka in Palestine; a Palestinian refugee camp in Lebanon; Hamido's city of birth, Beirut; and London, Hamido and Al Jazzar's current home. *On Akka's Shore* takes us on an exploration of the chaos of memory in relation to personal and collective history.

Slow Delay, dir. Therese Henningsen (2018; 16 min)
'You've got something I want, and I've got something you want,' he said. Twins Trevor and Raymond have lived together in New Cross for fifty years. They opened up their home to the director after she approached them on a bus and asked to film them.

The Filmmaker's House, dir. Marc Isaacs (2020; 75 min)
When the Filmmaker is told his next film must be about crime, sex or celebrity to get funded, he decides to take matters into his own hands and begins shooting a film in his home with people connected to his own life. The first characters we meet are two English builders whom Isaacs has employed to replace his garden fence and temporarily remove the barrier between him and his Pakistani neighbour. This introduces the central theme of hospitality – a theme that finds its ultimate expression when a homeless Slovakian man charms the Filmmaker's Colombian cleaner to let him into the house and tests everyone's ideas of the expectations and boundaries between host and guest. Blending documentary with fiction and wry humour with emotional intensity, Isaacs unfolds a story which – in its final act – asks pertinent questions about the nature of filmmaking itself.

Face Deal, dir. Mary Jiménez Freeman-Morris (2014; 29 min)
The director's 102-year-old father is afflicted with dementia. His memory loss raises questions about the nature of family lineage and identity. Who has she become for him? A Lynchian journey into illness where images unravel in their texture and words become visionary. 'Truth is in the eyes of the beholder.'

Next year we will leave, dir. Juliette Joffé (2021; 47 min)
Guided by a sentence from the director's childhood, she encounters three people in Paris: a collector of lost objects, a princess in Disneyland and a coffee seller. *Next year we will leave* is a reconciliation with Joffé's hometown through a dialogue with strangers. Through a mirroring effect, the first-person narrative echoes the stories of those filmed, questioning the possibilities of the documentary encounter.

Gallivant, dir. Andrew Kötting (1996; 104 min)
It is 1996 and filmmaker Andrew Kötting, his grandmother Gladys Morris (aged eighty-five) and his daughter Eden (seven) circumnavigate the whole coastline of the UK in a campervan. Eden has Joubert syndrome, a rare neurological disorder, and uses Makaton, a simple sign language, to communicate. As they travel around the edgelands, the family interact with various characters they meet on the way.

Here for Life, dir. Andrea Zimmerman & Adrian Jackson (2019; 87 min)
In a world and a city framed by finance and loss, ten Londoners make their wild and wayward way, arguing for their own terms of definition as they go: singular lives nudging towards a coexistence stronger than 'community'. On reclaimed land between two train tracks they find themselves on the right side of history, making their own wagers with the present tense and future hopes: with who has stolen what from whom, and how things might be fixed. Hesitant, troubled, open to wonder, bearing their wounds: so they, unruly, stage their lives. It is a heightened, often contradictory rite of passage; finding solidarity in resistance, without demands other than the right to go on.

ACKNOWLEDGEMENTS

First and foremost, we would like to warmly thank all of the contributors to this anthology, without whose work and inspiration we would not have conceived of this idea. A particular thanks to Gareth Evans for sowing the seed through his initial invitation to curate a film programme at Whitechapel Gallery, for his invested support, and for introducing us to our publisher Jess Chandler, whose thoughtful dedication to the project continues to be invaluable. Thank you to everyone who has either worked on or in other ways contributed to the development of the book: Aimee Selby, Rory Cook, Theo Inglis, Susu Laroche, Spiros Makris, Freya Finn Field-Donovan, Mandy Merck, Yuya Yokota, Elsa Lévy, Diana Duta, Thibaut Chuffart, Sidsel Meineche Hansen, Errol McGlashan, Maria Palacios Cruz, Mania Akbari, Sharna Pax (Tinne Zenner, Maeve Brennan), Invitations (Mark Aerial Waller, Judah Attille, Astrid Korporaal), Technecast; to Open City Documentary Festival for inviting us to develop the short course 'Documentary as Encounter'; and to Whitechapel Gallery for hosting the launch of this book. Thank you to the Danish Arts Council, the Humanities Arts and Research Institute (HARI) at Royal Holloway, University of London, and Flanders Literature, for their financial support.

'The Image of the Village' by Jon Bang Carlsen was originally published as 'Billedet af landsbyen' in *At opfinde virkeligheden: tekster om film og liv* (Copenhagen: Tiderne Skifter, 2017).

'Single Ticket' by Bruno De Wachter was originally published as 'Enkele reis' in *nY* in March 2013, www.ny-web.be.

'Towards a Transpersonal I' by Annie Ernaux was originally published as 'Vers un je transpersonnel' in *Autofictions & Cie*, ed. Serge Doubrovsky, Jacques Lecarme and Philippe Lejeune, Cahiers du RITM 6 (Nanterre: Université Paris X-Nanterre, 1993), reproduced here courtesy of Cahiers du RITM and Annie Ernaux.

A version of 'The Strangers within Us' by David MacDougall will be included in *The Art of the Observer: A Personal View of Documentary* (Manchester: Manchester University Press, 2022).

'Other Than Myself / My Other Self' by Trinh T. Minh-ha was first published in *Travellers' Tales: Narratives of Home and Displacement*, ed. George Robertson, Melinda Mash, Lisa Tickner, Jon Bird, Barry Curtis and Tim Putnam (London: Routledge, 1994), and reprinted in Trinh T. Minh-ha, *Elsewhere, Within Here: Immigration, Refugeeism and the Boundary Event* (London: Routledge, 2010)

'Strangers' by Toni Morrison was originally included as the introduction to *A Kind of Rapture* by Robert Bergman (New York: Pantheon Books, 1998), reproduced here with kind permission of the Estate of Chloe A. Morrison.

ABOUT PROTOTYPE

poetry / prose / interdisciplinary projects / anthologies

Creating new possibilities in the publishing of fiction and poetry through a flexible, interdisciplinary approach and the production of unique and beautiful books.

Prototype is an independent publisher working across genres and disciplines, committed to discovering and sharing work that exists outside the mainstream.

Each publication is unique in its form and presentation, and the aesthetic of each object is considered critical to its production.

Prototype strives to increase audiences for experimental writing, as the home for writers and artists whose work requires a creative vision not offered by mainstream literary publishers.

In its current, evolving form, Prototype consists of 4 strands of publications:

(type 1 — poetry)
(type 2 — prose)
(type 3 — interdisciplinary projects)
(type 4 — anthologies) including an annual anthology of new work, *PROTOTYPE*.

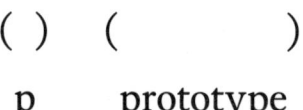